Jesus

Jesus—The Transforming Power of the Messiah
Copyright 2011 by Tony A. Metze

Printed by Createspace

Please check out Pastor Metze's other book, Biblical Leadership—The Fifth Frame. Send comments, suggestions or questions to: tonymetze@att.net

All Scripture quotations are from the Holy Bible, Revised Standard Version, New Revised Standard Version and New International Version.

Cover photo from www.dreamstime.com

ISBN: 1-4610-1005-5
ISBN-13: 9781461010050

Jesus

Forty Days with the Transforming Power of the Messiah

Rev. Tony A. Metze

2011

Dedication

This book is dedicated to my family: My wife, Christina, my daughter Melanie, her husband and my newest son Michael, my twin sons Mark and Christopher and my mother, Ella.

Table of Contents

Acknowledgements

I owe a debt of gratitude for all the people who have enabled me to fulfill my calling as an ordained pastor. While my reading of theological and pastoral administration books has continued through the years, each of the persons I have known is a book. Their lives have shaped me. Their faithfulness in living the gospel and supporting their congregation has enriched me spiritually. The life I have as a parish pastor is a blessing because of all of them. Each of the congregations I have served: Good Shepherd, Faith, St. James and St. Paul's have blessed me way beyond any expectations. My wife supports my work through her involvement in the life of the parish, but also in her encouragement for all that I must do.

My pastoral colleagues make ordained ministry invigorating. They provide feedback, support, encouragement and laughs for those times when I take myself too seriously. Of special note are the pastors of Cluster fourteen. We have had much fun and fellowship through the years as we planned each year of confirmation camp.

Will You Speak About Jesus?

Dr. David Yeago, professor of Theology at Lutheran Theological Southern Seminary, said on February 6, 2010 in an address to over seven hundred Lutherans, that in all his years of speaking to congregations about stewardship and a whole host of topics, no congregation ever asked him to speak about Jesus.[1] As shocking as it sounds, many congregations are interested in programs, purposeful living, a strategic plan for growing, conflict resolution, stewardship campaigns and social justice more than the person of Jesus. The American landscape is covered with high steeple buildings that exist to make Jesus known, but do people really know him. The uniqueness of Jesus is news worth sharing.

When I remember the day I delivered my first sermon to the congregation in which I grew up, one of the members asked pointedly, "Are you going to mention Jesus?" He asked in jest as if he expected my answer to be a resounding yes. Sadly, I paused for a moment as I wondered if Jesus was foremost in my prepared message.

Since that first sermon and probing question, it has become my mission to talk about Jesus. The church has many purposes and accomplishes many tasks, but Jesus is the center of Christianity. Christianity is not a religion; it is a revelation. It is not merely a practical guide for living or a philosophy of thought. Christianity is about the living God who clothed himself in flesh. It is all about Jesus.

Interestingly enough, heresies abound and are often cloaked in small patches of orthodoxy. While Jesus gets lip service, the truth is easily distorted. Michael Horton in his book, Christless Christianity, illustrates the many misrepresentations of the biblical Jesus. In his scathing criticism of a popular preacher he writes, "...his message represents a convergence of Pelagian self-help and Gnostic self-deification."[2]

Central to the message of an orthodox presentation of Jesus is a proper understanding of law and gospel. Simply, what the law of God demands, the gospel bestows. An imbalance in any proportion leads to Pelagianism in which one merits God's grace through one's efforts or Antinomianism in which one is free from the law. Bonheoffer called the latter cheap grace; it is forgiveness with no expectation of repentance. The law of God acts as a mirror in which we look to see our shortcomings, but also exists as a guide to enable the believer to live faithfully in response to the good news of Jesus.

While many wish to define Jesus on their terms making him into a wish granting Santa, Jesus is God in the flesh who calls all people to amend their lives and live under his rule. He does not exist to make us happy and give us our best life now, but transform us. While he promises abundant life, his abundance comes through worship, love of neighbor and service to one another and not by making us wealthy and rich.

This does not mean wealth is inherently evil. Many biblical saints possessed great wealth, but it is a gift of God and not some potential achievement linked to faithfulness.

Jesus does not relax the law to make us feel good. While we are granted his grace and forgiveness, we are not to presume upon his kindness. (Romans 2:4) The love of Christ and his love of us is intended to motivate us to live changed lives. Our lives are altered forever by the sacrifice of Jesus. This is not the same, however, as the popular prosperity preachers, one in particular who said, "If you simply obey his commands, he will change things in your favor."[3] God is not interested in our materialistic wish list as though we are self—centered narcissist. God wants to abide in us and make us a new creation in Christ.

In the midst of all the differences that exist, Christians are united in Jesus. It behooves us, however, to understand him properly. It is not enough to hear what people think about Jesus, we need a biblically formed picture of the Messiah. This book is one attempt at forming a coherent and biblically accurate picture of Jesus the Messiah. It is designed as a devotional to be read over a period of forty days. Biblical readings are assigned for each day along with an essay for reflection. The essays are intended to enable the reader to see how their lives intersect with the life changing power of the Messiah.

If you know Jesus as Messiah, then this book will enhance your growth and encourage you. If you are a seeker, this book can offer new insights and reflections on biblical readings and perhaps introduce you in a fresh and new way to the Messiah and his transforming power. Begin a new journey in search of the Jesus of scripture and his life changing power. Read, reflect, study and pray and meet Jesus again for the first time.

Day One
The Promise that
Prepares

Reading: Luke 3:1-18

We were traveling home from a family vacation in New Jersey south on the interstate and north of Washington D.C. I saw a billboard stating it was only several hundred miles to the infamous store "South of the Border." I laughed at the creativity and invitation of the signs. How many people see the signs advertising "South of the Border" and envision the most expansive store in the world?

The flashy billboards create eagerness and anticipation to visit this massively advertised store. I imagined that it must be an awesome place. Finally, we visited the store. It was apparent to me that the hyped expectation was far more interesting than what I experienced.

Many times we experience a spiritual and mental letdown. This occurs most markedly around holidays and especially at Christmas. Christmas is the season most known for its celebration of Jesus; the birth of the savior of the world. There are the preparations, the build up, and the anticipation, only to feel the familiar fatigue and disappointment that often follows in January. So often this happens during the holidays for those who, to use a cliché, put their eggs in one basket. That is to say, the letdown comes when we get excited and prepared for all the wrong things. We put our hopes and dreams in a perfect meal, or perfect gathering, or perfect gift, only to be disillusioned. Nothing ever comes together as perfectly or completely as we would like or plan during the holidays.

A rather rough and tumble sort of fellow gives us a glimpse of a cure for the holiday blues. His name is John the Baptist. John becomes the billboard for Jesus. John the Baptist holds up the sign for all to see. The critical verse in Luke chapter three is verse 2. The literal rendering of the Greek text says, "A Word of God happened upon John!" The C.E.O. of all advertisers, the God of creation delivered the ad, and he delivered it to John. It did not need editing. This word happened to John. He had the awesome responsibility of getting the word out.

John's succinct, simple, billboard message was this; "Proclaim a baptism of repentance for the forgiveness of sins. Prepare for the Lord!" John could do his job with the full confidence that Jesus was truly worth preparing for. John could herald the coming of Jesus knowing that when Jesus arrived on the scene, everyone could see the salvation of God. Unlike the famous "South of the Border" signs that promise more than they can truly deliver, John prepares for one who will deliver on his promises. John prepared the people for a person named Jesus.

Jesus was no mere moral teacher. Jesus was not simply another profound prophet. Jesus was not some slick marketing genius who could create curiosity. Jesus was and still is God. Jesus is God in flesh. The potter became part of the clay. Jesus is fully God and fully man. And Jesus will bring more than a trinket or two to put in your spiritual shopping basket.

Jesus has the power to forgive sins, the power to truly enable people to repent and turn from their destructive ways. Jesus is Prince of peace, Lord of lords, King of kings and the Mighty Counselor. John can only partially prepare us for one so awesome and so great. John began the preparation. It is incumbent upon us to continue the job. How will you prepare?

There is no question that we all need to prepare. The question, of course, is how. There are many big billboards making wild promises, but delivering very little in the end. Look around and you will see many products and promises that attempt to solve all your problems. There once was a television commercial with soft, soothing sound in the background. Front and center stood a man with arms uplifted. Water gently and smoothly trickled over his body. Then I heard the tag line, "the name of the car" for the salvation of your soul. It was shocking to see such powerful and holy religious images used to sell a car with the overriding message that the purchase of a car could somehow save you.

We prepare by being fiercely focused on the one who brings us true salvation. When we are taxed with the trivial treasures of gifts received, we should re-think the Christmas season and take every opportunity to refocus. We can tell the story of Saint Nicholas who was a Bishop of Myra in Turkey to illustrate that Christ is the true gift for all. We can fight the temptation to become consumed by consumerism. While we can enjoy a shopping expedition, we balance the buying with the sharing of time and treasures with Christian charitable organizations. We grow the true gifts of forgiveness, compassion and love. We share Jesus and his word of life in deeds and actions. We prepare by preparing our heart, our family, and our friends, for the best gift of all Jesus Christ, God's Son our Savior.

The billboard sign is clear, Jesus is the Messiah. He is the one who truly brings salvation and he can completely deliver on his promise of abundant and eternal life.

Day Two
The Refiner's Fire

Reading: Malachi 3: 1-4

In 1930 Dr. Olie Hallesby wrote, "Why I am a Christian"? In the Chapter, The Logic of Repentance, Hallesby writes about giving God your entire heart. He uses a most interesting analogy. He invites the men in his readership to call to mind their courtship days. So, I invite you to do the same. Remember when you gave your heart to your future wife. You said something like this, "I love you with all my heart." Do you remember? Suppose your bride to be responded in this manner, "Yes, I shall try. I shall do the best I can. I will live with you and work with you, make our home cozy, and save all I can for us and our children. But you must from the outset remember that I love somebody else. And you must allow me to continue to love him. I cannot live without him."[4]

Naturally, we see the absurdity and foolishness of such a proposal. No one can marry one person while giving their heart to another. Why do we expect anything different in our relationship with God? Is it enough for us to work with God, live with God, make our church cozy for God, bring our children up to know God, and not love God solely?

The scriptural book of Malachi sounds a strong warning about the coming of God's messenger. And the question is asked, who can endure the day of his coming and who can stand when he appears? The question hangs there for us to ponder. Perhaps we should make the question personal, can we endure the day of his coming? Can we stand when he appears?

In other words is there clutter in our lives? Are there spiritual cobwebs that appear to be hindering our growth in faith, a sleazy spiritual laziness? Are we simply too comfortable where we are that we see no need to be pushed or prodded to grow? Do we think that there is a time, any time in our life on earth when we spiritually graduate and get to the place we ought to be in our holy and devout life? Is there not a time when we can sit back, relax and say, I think I finally got Christian faith figured out?

Gail Sheehy coined the phrase "life passages." Think of the passages you have experienced. You marry, spend a few years getting to know one another, then have kids, then the kids go through adolescence, the kids move away, then you retire, and on and on it goes. Each stage is a passage in life. From being parents to being grandparents; some of you have progressed through quite a few of these passages, have you not? But what about our relationship with God, do we have passages, transitions, ups, downs?

Of course we do, but the one phase that is most dangerous, most destructive to faith is the "settled phase." I have done my part, you say, time for some-one else. Or, the idea that we have somehow arrived to full maturity in faith, and have learned all we need to learn, grown all we need to grow, heard all we need to hear, read all the books we need to read, and studied the Bible all we need to study; you get the idea. Life with Christ is a never ending journey, a never ending tension between already, but not yet. I am already a follower of Jesus, but I am not yet fully there.

That is why this reading from Malachi ought to unsettle us a bit. We need to be unsettled, we need to be shaken, and we need to be quaking, as it were, in our boots. Shall we be able to endure and stand at his coming? For you see the one who comes is like a refin-er's fire and a fullers' soap. He will sit as a refiner and purifier of silver, and he will purify the descendants of Levi and refine them like gold and silver.

When something is refined or purified, the im-purities are removed. What in your life keeps you from loving God fully and completely? Is it doubt, love of money, the relentless search for pleasure? The old tendency to behave like Adam and be disobedient to God is what we call sin. This innate desire to follow our own will continues to reside in us and plague us even after we experience salvation with Christ. But, God can move our wills and get us out of the way.

I cannot will my way to God or reason my way to God, but somewhere along the way I can get out of the way. We can submit our will, our heart, our soul, our thoughts and all that we are to the one who will refine and purify, today, tomorrow and indeed every waking moment. He comes to purify and refine you, me and all who call upon his name.

And we can ask but one thing really; Jesus, help me to love you fully and completely. There is one encouraging word in this reading from Malachi—"until." It is in verse three in this reading, "...refine them like gold and silver, until..." Until has a persistent sound to it. It sounds like Jesus will refine and purify us until we are ready to present offerings in righteousness. In other words, we will come before the Lord and offer ourselves and offer everything we have and offer it in righteousness. We offer everything until our hearts are right and in tune with God. And it will be pleasing to Jesus. May Jesus the Messiah give you strength and love and purify you for holy living.

Day Three
"Do You Have A Rusty Life?"

Reading: Mark 1:1-8

I have a 1968 Ford, Grand Torino. My dad gave it to me in 1977. I was glad to get it. I still own it. It is somewhat of an expensive toy, I suppose. Some years back, I decided that if it ever would be repainted, I would have to do it myself. Partly because of the cost involved. And so, I asked a number of friends with painting expertise, solicited some expert advice, and went to work in my spare minutes. I spent ten minutes here and fifteen minutes there sanding the rust away.

Then, after the sanding, I sprayed on primer. Much to my surprise, a few weeks later, surface rust began to reappear in the places I had sanded and primed. I had forgotten one very important part. I should have put a rust preventative on before the primer. Preparation is everything in the car painting business. No matter how great the paint, if the preparation is shoddy, then the paint job will eventually be shoddy.

Preparation is everything in the Christian's journey. The gospel of Mark begins with preparations. Mark does not begin with a birth story. Immediately, we are thrust on the scene with a wild sounding man with a wild diet and radical clothes. It is John the Baptist whose role in life, and a very good one I might add, is to prepare the way for Jesus.

He prepares the crowd with repentance and confession and baptism, and by proclaiming Christ as the Mighty one. John knows that it takes more than a coat of paint to make something new. Rust will grow in the life of an individual if they merely scratch the surface of God's words. All the glitter and fancy trimming that adorns our houses during Christmas do not make the difference. Rust can still grow in our lives and the lives of many others if we fail to prepare.

Christianity is not a religion of rules and regulations. It is a life dedicated to following Jesus the Christ. Repentance, confession, baptism; these are all part of the preparation process. And if we lay a good foundation, then we can shine in good times and in bad.

How often I grieve for those who cry out to God for help in the midst of crisis when they have no foundation. Suddenly, they come face to face with a problem that is overwhelming. They need encouraging words from scripture, such as the 23rd psalm, but they are so unfamiliar with the Bible they do not even know where to turn. They want the full support of the church, but they have not participated in a family of faith for months, maybe even years. In essence, they expect their faith to shine like new paint, but they have failed to do any sanding at all. They want to know the Good Shepherd of which their childhood memories evoke, but they have long since wandered from the pasture.

The shiny lives of other Christians you may know did not come easily. Those I have known over the years who wear perpetual smiles have also known the hardships and the storms, but the difference is they are prepared. The substance, the real toughness comes from the sanding. Richard Niebuhr, author and theologian said it like this, "A God without wrath brings people without sin into a kingdom without pain through the ministrations of a Christ without a cross."[5]

Are you prepared? Do you not want for yourself and your friends and neighbors something more, something real? Do you want a faith that is living, active, and relevant to your life not only on Sunday but every day? Then get to know Jesus the Christ who was born in a stable not safe and secure in some shiny cradle couched between stain glass windows. You want Jesus the God/ Man; the crucified one. You need the one whose blood stained body enables us to be coated with the paint of righteousness. You need the one who through his suffering enables you to shine like the sun.

You want to shine? You want a real faith? Then, a congregational family is the place to begin. There you will be among friends. Pray for God to call you to the right place. For, it is in the family of faith that you can prepare. It is in the gathered people of God where you worship and glorify God your maker. The church is not a social club. It is not a place to be seen so as to make a good impression. It is a place to be fed, nourished and shined.

Jesus wants to start to work on you. He wants to sand away the rough spots and smooth out the hard places. He wants to prepare you for eternity and he wants to start at this very moment. Confession is good for the soul. Repentance means turning your life around and upside down. Today is the day for preparation. Not tomorrow, nor a week from now, today is the day of salvation. Ask Jesus to start the sanding. Allow Jesus to draw you into reading the word and praying fervently. Make time to worship regularly and to do so with sincerity and energy.

Today, my 1968 Torino looks great, but it took a tremendous amount of time and much patience. I prepared. I invite you to prepare your life. Remember poor preparation leads to rusty lives. Remember, also, faith is not merely some shiny paint that covers the blemishes of our lives. Faith helps us endure the ups and the downs and the blemishes along the way. Faith is, simply, Jesus Christ. Faith is the living relationship in a Lord we call upon to prepare us. Faith in Christ prevents the permanently damaging rust. Come Lord Jesus!

Day Four
The Gospel
According To
Mary

Reading: Luke 1:39-45

Some scholars speculate about what would happen if we suddenly discovered a fifth Gospel written by Mary, the mother of our Lord. Would it be a saga of suffering? Would it focus on the bitterness of being blessed? Mary's life is a testimony to the fact that to be favored by God is not always a "bed of roses".

As a teenager she was pregnant and unwed. She had to face the puzzled glances of Joseph and probably some embarrassing questions of a small town community. Early in her pregnancy she walked a three-day journey to visit her cousin Elizabeth. Late in her pregnancy she made the difficult trip to Bethlehem where she gave birth to her baby in a barn. Soon after the child was born, she, her baby, and her husband Joseph had to flee for their very lives into Egypt.

When her son was twelve years old he denounced his family responsibilities, saying that, "He must be about his father's business." Rather, he would become an itinerant preacher like his cousin, John. When he was a successful teacher he publicly rebuffed his mother saying that his followers were his family.

Mary saw her son betrayed and denied by his friends. She saw him accused, tried and found guilty of treason against God and country. She saw him die like a common criminal on a cross. In spite of the fact that she was a witness to his resurrected body, she could never drive from her mind the terrifying vision of his agonizing death—dying by degrees with nails piercing the body that was flesh of her flesh.

Mary knew first hand the tragic consequences of being favored by God. Therefore, we would expect that her version of the story of Jesus would be a sad, bad news gospel. However, if this reading is any indication of Mary's mind we would have an altogether different direction to our speculation concerning a gospel Mary might write.

Consider her words in the reading often known as the Magnificat, the Latin phrase for magnify. Mary's words are a hymn of praise and joy. Interestingly, when the believers in the early church first used this canticle in their liturgies, it was called, "The Gospel of Mary." According to this we can be certain that if Mary had written a gospel it would not be a tragic rehearsal of her sufferings but a good news gospel.

Unlike most of us, Mary did not concentrate on her hardships or complain to God about her pain;

rather she sang a song about God the Almighty who has done "great things for me". How could Mary rejoice and praise God in the midst of her afflictions and adversities, her trials and tribulations? The reading reveals to us it was because Mary focused her attention not on herself and her misery, but on God and his mercy.

As a new mother Mary knew that pain is the birth pangs of a new life. Mary caught a vision that a great hope was being born in a womb of this world. A new age of faith was dawning. The proud and mighty were being shaken from their high positions of power. She saw the poor and lowly exalted. She saw the hungry fed. She saw the lost, lonely, unloved people of this world being welcomed into the caring arms of a comforting God.

She had been visited by a vision and it so vibrated her very being that her words flowed forth in poetry and song, "My soul magnifies the Lord and my spirit rejoices in God my savior." And Mary is not alone. All the helpless people of history have sung hymns of joy when they have been captured by a vision of hope. So, reflect upon the Magnificat, a hymn of praise and glory to God.

For us, hope is no mere speculation; our hope is certain expectation. For us hope is no pie-in-the-sky-by-and-by kind of hope; our hope is a babe-in-a-barn-born-to-die kind of hope. Therefore, sing with a loud voice, "Come Lord Jesus!"

Day Five
How about a sign?

Reading: Isaiah 7:10 -14

For only a moment pretend you are on the once famous game show the 25,000 dollar pyramid. Here are some clues; Yield, Stop, Flashing lights, Children, Shadows, Snakes. You might guess such things as; things you see on the road, things that convey a message, things you see at a railroad crossing, or things you see in the Bible. The correct answer would be signs.

Signs are important throughout the Holy Scripture. Abraham asks God to give him a sign that he will inherit the land that God promised him. The sign is a covenant ceremony in Chapter 15 of Genesis. A rather bizarre sounding ceremony in which animals are cut in two and a torch is passed between them. Moses asks God to give him a sign so that folks will know God actually appeared to him. God tells him to cast down his rod and it will turn into a serpent. Gideon asks for a sign so that he will know God is really talking to him. Gideon asks that a fleece of wool be wet and the ground dry and then a second time asks that the ground be wet and the fleece dry. King Hezekiah asks for a sign for the Lord to heal him and God grants him a sign that a shadow will go back ten steps.

In the book of Isaiah we read about another King, King Ahaz of Judah who was succeeded by King Hezekiah. However, unlike the others who ask for a sign, King Ahaz refuses to do so. In Isaiah Chapter 2:8 we are told that Judah, of which Ahaz is king, is remembered for its idolatrous practices. If you look in 2 Kings 16: 2-3 you will read, "Ahaz was twenty years old when he became king, and he reigned in Jerusalem sixteen years. Unlike David his father, he did not do what was right in the eyes of the Lord his God. He walked in the ways of the kings of Israel and even sacrificed his son in the fire."

Ahaz, as it appears, is not one who trusts in the Lord. He says he does not ask for a sign because he does not wish to put the Lord to the test. Really now, Ahaz! You think he refuses to ask for a sign because he does not want to put the Lord to the test. Abraham asks for a sign, Moses, Gideon, and so do many others. Ahaz resists because Ahaz does not want a sign from God. Ahaz does not want to hear from God. Ahaz does not want to hear what the Lord has to say to him.

In verse nine of this same Chapter of Isaiah, Isaiah tells Ahaz not to make alliances with other nations, but says to him, "If you do not stand firm in your faith, you will not stand at all." Ahaz refuses to ask for a sign. Ahaz refuses to trust in God. Ahaz puts his trust and the nation of Judah in the hands of Tiglath-pileser III, King of Assyria.

No doubt we could excuse Ahaz as a victim of circumstance. No doubt we could find excuses for his weakness and lack of trust. After all, a whole people depended on his decision. An alliance, something which appeared to promise immediate relief, looked better than a mere word from the prophet. No doubt we could bypass his failings and try to find a bright side. But the fact remains, Ahaz did not want a sign from God, and yet God gave him a sign anyway.

Maybe he refuses the sign because he did not want to wait. Perhaps he thought accepting the sign opened him to God's direction and Ahaz wanted to make his own decisions. How easy it is to fall for temptations as did Ahaz. It is true that temptations often come our way that are subtle and insidious. We may see immediate satisfaction and be drawn to the solution that is instantaneous.

Christianity is not a quick fix. Following Christ was never meant to be easy. Trusting God is stepping out in faith. It means listening to his word and not acting as Ahaz and trusting in a foreign alliance, which no doubt appeared to be the easy way out. Growing in faith is a risky adventure, but one which always offers rewards.

God has given us a sign in Jesus Christ. Jesus is a sign that points our way to effective living. This does not mean that we find in Christ instant satisfaction or on the spot solutions. Christianity is a lifestyle that requires responsibility and trust. Unfortunately, many people opt for short term solutions. Faith in Christ is a long term, lifelong adventure. God invites us to embrace the sign of a baby born in a manger and the life of faith. He asks us to grow in faith and trust in his guidance, even in those times when we may feel as if God is guiding us into unexpected or unknown places.

How about you? Will you dare to ask God for a sign? Will you ask that the sign of Jesus be born anew in your heart and life today? Will you grow with Jesus and not look for the easy out?

Day Six
A Pig Pen
Attitude

Reading: Luke 2:1-20

Do you read the comic strip Peanut's? If you do, you will recall that there is a character by the name of Pig-Pen. Pig pen is portrayed surrounded by a cloud of dust. Why is he this way? Have you ever wondered? Is it because he is dirty or is there some symbolic meaning? I am not going to be able to solve that puzzle for you.

Have you ever been like pig pen? Now before you answer that question yes or no, let me elaborate a bit. Certainly the question does not mean to ask about your bathing practices. Rather, what air do you bring with you? What do people say when they see you coming down the sidewalk or hallway? Hopefully, they do not run. Truth is each of us is a mixture of good news and bad news, good days and bad days, ups and downs. But, do you not desire something more from life than a humdrum existence? Do you not want happiness, joy, and peace in your life? This is the message of Jesus Christ. Jesus comes to bring us a deep and abiding joy and peace. As the apostle Paul writes, a peace that passes all human understanding, in other words a peace and joy from God.

One parishioner I grew to love deeply greeted everyone with his favorite phrase, "It's a beautiful day!" He greeted me so much with those words that a subtle conditioning, as psychologists would call it, took effect. That is to say he conditioned people to expect something positive when they were around him. Now this man had health problems that could have caused anyone to develop a sour attitude, and I am sure that he had down days. But, he conditioned me to hear the words, it's a beautiful day. Do you not deeply desire an attitude such as that?

The first thing people do is run to the store for the latest book that purports how to find happiness. Counselors, advisors, celebrities, and a whole host of others offer the latest way, and what often becomes the latest fad, to find satisfaction in life. We are thankful to God for our health care professionals and for all who help us when the burdens of life come crashing down upon us. We should turn to these professionals when depression and despair strikes a heavy blow. But also, may we draw deeply from the well of hope in Jesus as a primary place to begin.

Allow the story of Jesus to permeate your being. Hear in a fresh new way the proclamation of the angel, "For behold I bring you good news of a great joy which will come to all the people." Listen to the angels sing, "Glory to God in the highest, and on earth peace among men with whom he is pleased." Ponder the actions of the shepherds as they returned, "glorifying and praising God for all they had heard and seen." Experience the joy. Believe it with all your heart. It is a beautiful day when we hear this story again for the first time.

Dr. Hallesby in his little book, "Why I am a Christian," offers these words of advice when one experiences the salvation of Jesus Christ. He writes "You experience Jesus as a present, blessed reality. In the moment that you with your new spiritual senses apprehend the invisible world of grace in which the cross is the center, in that moment a new life dawns upon your whole inner and outward being. Your soul is filled with unspeakable joy and with that peace which passes all understanding."[6]

This joy that is deep and lasting comes only through Jesus. You see you cannot muster up the joy that Jesus gives. You cannot acquire this with money or fame. You cannot buy it. Jesus gives it. And more importantly Jesus gives himself. There is no other way to salvation. Jesus is the way, the truth and the life. Every day is an opportunity for us to experience fully the birth of Jesus in our world and in our lives.

In the movie, The Nativity, it was amazing to see the look on Joseph's face as he sat by the baby Jesus as the shepherds and wise men came. The actor in the movie did an excellent job of displaying a look of wonder and surprise. His face conveyed this feeling of, "wow look at all of these people coming to see this baby," it was if he were wondering why?

They came to Jesus because the lowly shepherds and wise men knew that Jesus was the one of whom the prophets spoke. They knew Jesus was the one who gives his people peace and joy.

So when you feel like pig pen, bring your hurts to Jesus. Bring the surrounding dust clouds of doubt and despair to Jesus. Then believe in Jesus with all of your heart, mind and soul. Experience Jesus, by reading and hearing the wonderful story of his life and you will have not only a beautiful day, but also a beautiful life.

Day Seven
Babies and
Alligators

Reading: Colossians 1:18-19

A trip to Riverbanks Zoo in Columbia, South Carolina, during the Christmas season reveals a beautiful display of lights. My reflection on one trip called to mind a certain seeming inconsistency. There are lights, Christmas music, crowds dressed in reds, all looking quite festive and then all the precious animals. You know the small, cuddly and cute ones. All of it so appropriately placed together, except you see for the alligator. Now I have nothing against alligators, but somehow they seem out of place in the mixture of all that beauty. For one thing they are not very approachable. When visiting Riverbanks, I have heard no-one say, "Isn't that ten foot gator a real cutie."

No one, or should I say no one who thinks clearly, is interested in approaching a 20 foot alligator. They are unapproachable. Contrast this with something or someone to whom you willingly draw near. I am drawn to birds and find them alluring. All of you would say that about a baby. Only observe what happens when a small infant is brought into a room, even the curmudgeons among us are quick to walk over, look into those precious little eyes, pinch a cheek and say, "oh how cute!"

Alligators and babies offer quite a contrast. And lest you think I am lost in the zoo, allow me to ask this question. What is your image of God? Is God like an alligator, fierce and unapproachable? Or is God like a baby?

Luke recounts the story of the birth of Jesus in the second Chapter of the book that bears his name. This story is set in a specific time. This is the time of Caesar Augustus and Quirinius was governor of Syria. This is the place of Bethlehem. This scene is very familiar to us. We see a betrothed couple, a manger, cattle, shepherds, angels and one tiny baby boy infant. We also see adults and children alike pinching this baby on the cheek and saying, "Isn't he so cute?" This baby Jesus is God. Yes, he is God. This is the one and only God. This is the God who with a handful of nothing created a vast and magnificent universe. And then he created you.

Cast aside whatever images of God you have that portray God as a fierce, bearded, elderly man wielding thunderbolts or waiting to pounce on those who do wrong. Look into the manger and see God, the God of flesh, the God of love, the God who is approachable. And yes, even more, not only approachable, but a God who draws us to him like a magnet, like any other infant that attracts attention, except more so. This baby

Savior pulls, attracts, and draws us close, and in him we see the face of God.

Paul writes in Colossians 1:18-19; "He is the head of the body, the church; he is the beginning, the first-born from the dead, so that he might come to have first place in everything. For in him all the fullness of God was pleased to dwell." All the fullness of God dwells in Jesus. We see all the fullness of God in the face and person of Jesus, like an approachable baby.

During the Christmas season when churches read the story of Jesus birth and many people celebrate the season of Christmas, remember that Christmas is much more than gifts and bows; it is the incarnation of God, God becoming flesh, and God approaching us. Even the Grinch of Dr. Seuss fame learned that Christmas is more than bows and such.

And the Grinch, with his Grinch-feet ice-cold in the snow, stood puzzling and puzzling: "How could it be so?" "It came with out ribbons! It came without tags!" "It came without packages, boxes or bags!" And he puzzled three hours, till his puzzler was sore. Then the Grinch thought of something he hadn't before! "Maybe Christmas," he thought, "doesn't come from a store." "Maybe Christmas, perhaps, means a little bit more!"[7]

Yes, Christians celebrate Christmas once a year, but the season is so much more. In all the festivity of the season of Christmas there are also the fears, worries, and concerns. There are many people living with heavy burdens. Jesus asks that you cast all your cares on him. The season of Christmas is about Jesus. And

Jesus is approachable. He is Emmanuel, God with us. May Jesus bless your life and may all of your life be lived with the greatest gift of all Jesus the Messiah.

Day Eight
Be Born in Us!

Reading: John 1:1-18

Most, if not all of you have taken photographs and enjoyed viewing them. Of course, some of you use digital technology and view the pictures on your computer. Few people, if any, have portraits made. A picture is an exact rendering, whereas a portrait is an interpretation, though often done quite well. In the New Testament there are four gospels, four portraits if you will of Jesus, four authors each presenting the truth, but giving us another perspective, a view from a different angle if you will.

Matthew, the first gospel, presents Jesus as the giver of the new law. Jesus is the Messiah who possesses the authority of God as judge and redeemer. Thus Matthew gives us the story of the sheep and the goats. Mark is in a hurry, or so it seems. Mark is interested in no frills and few stories. He captures the Lord's power. Mark sees Jesus as the Son of God and Son of Man come to earth to do battle with the forces of evil. Luke sees Jesus with compassion. Luke shares stories of Jesus concern for all people. He is the good shepherd seeking to save and heal all the lost and broken of the world.

And then there is John. John includes no birth narrative. John does not record the visit of the shepherds or the presentation of the gifts from the wise men. John paints a portrait that is broad in its scope. John is concerned with how the birth of Jesus impacts the entire history of the world. John communicates that the Word was in the beginning. The Word became flesh. While Luke and Matthew tell us of the birth of Jesus and so indicate that Jesus was born in human flesh, John says the Word became flesh. John indicates in grand style that God is one of us and wishes to walk with us and be with us.

Dr. Hoefler, former professor of preaching at Lutheran Theological Southern Seminary and now a member of the Church triumphant, related the story of a young soldier in Korea who burst into tears and shouted, "Chaplain, pray for me! We jump off in an hour. Pray that I will come back alive." When the soldier had calmed down a bit, the chaplain replied, "Son, I can't offer that kind of prayer. You are going where grenades and bombs will be exploding. Some soldiers are not going to come back. I cannot ask God to favor you more than he does the other soldiers. But I tell you what I can do—I will go with you."

This is the difference between communication and communion. God indeed does communicate with us, but so much more God goes with us through the turbulence of our lives to bring us his very self. God communes with us in Jesus. This is the radical message of John's gospel. "The Word became flesh and dwelt among us." This is why Christians use and adore the word incarnation so much. This word means in the flesh. No other faith and no other religion can lay hold to this claim. The particular message of our faith is that the infinite creator, all powerful God became a human being. But the message is so much more. God became flesh on earth and lived on earth in order to live in us.

Consider the beautiful Christmas hymn by Phillip Brooks, O Little Town of Bethlehem. In verse 4 Brooks includes these words, "O Holy Child of Bethlehem, Descend to us we pray; Cast out our sin, and enter in, be born in us today." Cast out our sin and enter in, be born in us. This is the continuation of the incarnation. Christ is born in human flesh and Christ is born in us. Paul argues this point in Romans Chapter 6 when he says that we are united with Christ. And indeed if Christ is to be born in us, then there are not only four portraits of our savior's life but so many more. Your life is the fifth portrait.

As we live the faith, we present to the world a picture of what the Christian looks like. And we pray that our lives will give witness to the baby born in the manger, the baby born for the salvation of the whole world.

Near the end of WWII a distinguished, well known bishop of the Church of England visited the amputee's ward at an army hospital. His congregation was young men in wheelchairs and on stretchers and crutches, all minus arms or legs. The Bishop preached about the power of God in Jesus not only to heal broken bodies, but to make whole crippled minds, minds that had resigned themselves to the seemingly useless life of being handicapped. The Bishop preached his heart out, but when he finished, he knew his words had failed to break through the barrier of their defeat. The faces of the men showed little hope. Then the Bishop walked out into the center of the chancel and began to remove his robes. He took off his shirt and even his pants. The soldiers were shocked. But underneath the soldiers saw a man who lacked a left arm and a right leg. In the place of these missing limbs was an endless number of complicated braces, pulleys and belts. Then the Bishop pronounced the benediction.

Young lives were changed. The soldiers even requested that a picture of the bishop be hung in every ward of the hospital to remind them of what God can do. This brings new meaning to "the word became flesh and dwelt among us." Christ is born in us in order that we might be a new creation.

Day Nine
Three Hikers

Reading: Luke 9: 28-36

Flying Brian is an interesting person. Flying Brian is not his real full name, but his trail handle, the name that Appalachian Trail hikers give to one another. Some years ago Brian decided to establish a record for the fastest hike on the Appalachian Trail. He averaged 40 miles per day walking or perhaps he was running! Who knows? The question I have is simple. If hiking is fun and you enjoy the climb up a mountain, why do it in such a hurry?

Plenty of folks escape every year to the Great Smoky Mountains. At last count some 8 million people visit this park every year. But when people go to the mountains they expect to relax and stay a while. This reading is about a few hikers who went up a mountain. Some wanted to stay a while. Let's take a closer look.

There are four people going on this little hike. Jesus, the one we profess as the Messiah, the Chosen one by God, leads three of his followers up a high mountain. The three, Peter, James and John, are known by many as three of Jesus' closest followers. What happens on the mountain is nothing less than miraculous. Their little excursion into the wilderness turns into an extraordinary walk into the supernatural.

This reading says Jesus was transfigured. Now that is one of those thousand dollar church words. Webster defines it this way, "to give a new and typically exalted or spiritual appearance to, to transform outwardly" The biblical text goes on to say that his clothes became dazzling white and that Moses and Elijah appeared beside Jesus.

Now picture yourself in this scene. What would you do and how would you react? Most of us would be frightened, just as the disciples reacted. The story says, "They were terrified." Peter and the others are terrified, but not so terrified that Peter did not at least ask if it were time to pitch the tents. He says, "Rabbi, it is good for us to be here; let us make three dwellings, one for you, one for Moses, and one for Elijah."

It is time to set up camp. This means in effect that it is time to stay overnight or perhaps even for a few days. After Peter suggests it is time to settle in and pitch tents, there are some shocking words that shake their mountain. There is a cloud and then a heavenly voice, "This is my Son, the Beloved; listen to him!" One other time the disciples hear this voice and it is at the baptism of Jesus. On that occasion the voice says, "Thou are my beloved Son; with thee I am well pleased." Whether at the baptism or the transfiguration, what is crystal clear is the pronouncement that Jesus is the Son of God.

Now this is quite the mountain top revelation. Confirmed once again for these three hikers is the radical pronouncement that Jesus, the man with whom they have walked and talked, is the son of the infinite creator of the universe. Perhaps all of us might do well to reflect on the meaning of this event. Who is Jesus, and more importantly, what does he mean for you and me?

I first heard this story from a lecture by Patrick Allit, the professor of history at Emory University. The story is told of the Seneca and Sitka Indian tribes. These two tribes were engaged in a violent war against each other. Days and days wear on and finally the Seneca Chief calls across the plain that separated the two tribes and pleads with the Sitka chief for a truce. The Seneca chief argues that winter is approaching and they need time to prepare, the war is a distraction. The Sitka chief argues that he cannot end the war because the Seneca Indians have killed more of the Sitka braves. Once more the Seneca Chief asks for an end to the violence, pleading for peace. Finally, the Sitka warrior chief states that there can be no end to the war as long as they have killed more of his braves. There must be an equal blood account for the war to end, says the Sitka chief. You have killed at least ten more of my men. At which point the Seneca chief says, do you agree that I am worth at least ten of your warriors? To which the Sitka chief says of course. So, bravely the Seneca Chief walks out into the open field and says, then take me, and let's end this war. Immediately, the Seneca Chief is killed and the war is over.

Jesuit priests came to this country very early and shared this story with the Native Americans in their attempts to bring them to Jesus Christ. This, they said, is what Jesus does for you and me. He offered his life for you and me. We understand that Jesus is the Son of God who died on a cross to settle the blood account. He arose from death that we might have eternal life.

Day Ten
A Spiritual
Triptik

Reading: Isaiah 43: 1-7

How many of you are familiar with the AAA Triptik? These maps provided to members of AAA take you on a journey. There are fold out pages that provide a close up of one city and the roads one should travel. Will you join me as we travel on a spiritual triptik?

The journey begins with God. In the beginning God created. It is the nature of God to create. God made the earth, the sea, the animals, in essence the entire universe. It is God who put together the double helix we call DNA. It is God who put into place the processes to fashion DNA in such a way that those basic building blocks are used to make you and me. God creates.

Isaiah 43:1 "But now thus says the LORD, he who created you, O Jacob, he who formed you, O Israel: Do not fear, for I have redeemed you; I have called you by name, you are mine."

Consider for your spiritual journey not only did God create you, but created and redeemed you. God set you apart and called you by name. You belong to God. This is your beginning to spiritual depth and happiness—to know, to repeat like a mantra, to drill into your minds, hearts, souls, this one important fact, that you begin your journeys knowing that God made you, redeems you and calls you by name.

The second leg of the journey is the detour. Everyone knows about driving to and through large cities. Have you ever been to Atlanta, Georgia? Can you recall going on a long trip and encountering road construction? In other words no journey is complete, unfortunately, without some wrong turns, detours, or bad weather. In every life a little rain must fall.

There is not a single person who has not at some time or another encountered spiritual hardship. Whether it was doubt, despair, confusion about your beliefs, frustration with a fellow Christian or even the body of Christ—the Church itself, all of us know some kind of hurt. Many of our problems are at their root—spiritual problems. How we handle our money is a spiritual issue. How we handle our free time is a spiritual issue. How we handle our doubts is a spiritual issue. How we deal with conflict is a spiritual issue. How we handle frustration is a spiritual issue. Everything ultimately is about our relationship with God.

The question is what do you do when you come to a detour or encounter a bump in the road? Many people play the blame game. They reason that it must be somebody else's fault. They blame God, blame the neighbor, blame the politicians, and think someone else must be to blame for their problem! Rather, why not ponder when the problems come along in your spiritual journey that God is with you.

"When you pass through the waters, I will be with you; and through the rivers, they shall not overwhelm you; when you walk through fire you shall not be burned, and the flame shall not consume you." (Isaiah 43:2)

There is no doubt in my mind that when the people heard these words they thought back to the story of the Exodus from Egypt. They probably remembered the stories of their ancestors who told them about crossing the Red Sea. In other words, when they took their journey to the Promised Land—they knew that God was with them. Do you believe this? Do you believe that God is with you? Comfort yourself with these words, "I can do all things through Christ who gives me strength." (Philippians 4:13)

The third leg of the journey is the meeting with friends and family. Perhaps you have recently visited a family member. Maybe each year you have made a New Year resolution to visit your family more often. Can you imagine taking a trip to your brother or sisters home town, say California for instance, and not visiting your family? Would someone drive for days to where their family resides and not visit their family?

In the spiritual journey, the body of Christ, the local congregation is your family. You need to commit yourself to visit God's family, God's house of prayer, regularly. Regularly does not mean once a month. You need the fellowship, the prayers, the hymns, the words of God, and the sacraments. You need the church. To not worship regularly is like going to the Grand Canyon, but never getting out of the hotel to take a look at it. To look at the Grand Canyon is to bask in the wonder and majesty of God and His Creation.

"Because you are precious in my sight, and honored, and I love you, I give people in return for you, nations in exchange for your life. Do not fear, for I am with you; I will bring your offspring from the east, and from the west I will gather you; I will say to the north, "Give them up," and to the south, "Do not withhold; bring my sons from far away and my daughters from the end of the earth" (Isaiah 43:4-6) God wants to gather us together in worship because we are precious in his sight.

The fourth leg of the journey is to return home. As a vacation ends with a return home, our spiritual journey ends when we return to our final home. It ends where it begins. "Everyone who is called by my name, whom I created for my glory, whom I formed and made" (Isaiah 43:7)

God made us and formed us for eternity. As we gather with other Christians in worship, we prepare for our day to day journey and our eternal journey. Is it not about time you secure a spiritual triptik and prepare for your Christian journey?

Day Eleven
Spiritual Briars

Reading: Isaiah 43: 18-19

This story seems so unbelievable, but it is true. Kevin was hunting. He made his way through the woods with ease, until he decided to push through some thick brush. Think about it for a moment. Why travel along the easy path when you can try to plow over some bushes—it's more fun is it not. Anyway, Kevin did just that. He made his way through the bushes and in the bushes were briars. One of the branches lunged into Kevin's left nostril! To make matters worse, Kevin tried to pull out the briar which was firmly planted in his nose. Bleeding profusely, Kevin came out of the woods with a briar up his nose. It took a hospital visit to remove the intrusive and unwanted branch.

Nowhere have I ever heard of someone getting a briar up their nose. But it is true that all of us have encountered briars, and I am not talking about the kind encountered in the woods. Rather, there are spiritual briars that tear our flesh and rip our hearts. Some would even say that we live in a wilderness. Sure there are the good deeds. There are the people who share their resources every day. We are a nation of just and fair people. There are plenty of opportunities to open our eyes and count the many blessings of our lives and our land.

But make no mistake, there are briars. And there are the daily dry blasts of liberal leaning people who dismantle the Christian faith. An article in the Lutheran magazine recounted the story of a Bishop in the Methodist church who was defrocked. In a speech at a theological school he said that he did not believe in the virgin birth, the bodily resurrection of Jesus, or the role of Jesus in our salvation. And this man was a Bishop. A movie starring Kevin Spacey included a snide comment about William Bennett's book, The Book of Virtues. Had it not been for a movie review in the Wall Street Journal that pointed out the small insult, most would have missed it.

And that is the sneaky way of the spiritual briars. They infiltrate our souls so that we may not even notice the slippery slope that leads to despair and doubt. There are those who belittle the Christian faith and pick and tear at it repeatedly.

But sadly those on the outside are not our greatest enemy. Sometimes we are the enemies of briar free living. That which picks at our attempts to grow in faith is not always those things that attack from the outside. It is often our tendency to look back at our past and grieve over our past mistakes. There is always a time for repentance. There is always time to be sorry for our sins, but there is also a time to put the past in the past.

Because if we live with our past as if it were a ghost waiting to haunt us at every corner, then we are not going to grow as disciples of Jesus Christ. To grow we need to move on.

Isaiah prophesies to a people who are reeling in despair from the destruction of the Babylonians. As far as the people are concerned, there is no hope. Their past haunts. And to that Isaiah says, "Do not remember the former things, or consider things of old." Hear those liberating words. Listen to God's word for you, forget the past and put it behind you.

What is it that haunts you? Is it a past marked by wild and reckless living? Were you the child of an alcoholic or abusive parent? There are individuals who daily carry the hurt of a past relationship and the hurt of past sins. These are spiritual briars because they hurt us deeply and rip and tear at our growth as God's people.

Think about it. What sins stick in your soul like a briar that will not let go? What weak parts of your life does the devil continue to prod and pick at in hopes of tearing you down? Sometimes we feel surrounded by briars and lost in a wilderness. Too many times we succumb to the temptation to be a victim of our past. You know the old song of victim hood. It is the tendency to think that because of our past we can never fully be what we want to be. This is the lie of our culture. We may never be what we want to be, but with God it is a different story. God can make us his beloved children. God can make us new hearts. A victim attitude can lock someone in old bad habits as they begin to believe that the old hurts will never go away and will continually hold them back. Hear these words, "Do not remember the former things." "I am about to do a new thing!" "I will make a way in the wilderness and rivers in the desert."

Believe this word. Believe that God can bring water in the middle of the parched and dry soul. Believe that God can refresh and renew a troubled and contrite spirit. Believe that Jesus Christ can and will bear your sins. The word says it clearly, "and I will not remember your sins."

Isaiah tells the people of God who are in despair over the past and the damage to their land and their culture; I will blot out your transgressions for my sake. For God's sake, we know his name as Jesus. God blotted out his own son. God turned his back on his own son in a moment. Jesus died, truly died and in that moment all your sins died. And as Jesus was raised from the dead, we too might be raised to a new life. Today is a good day to lay it all down and pick up a new life. That is God's wish for you.

Day Twelve
A Holy
Hospitality

Reading: Mark 1: 40-45

Do you have a front porch? Some years ago, it was common for families to sit on the front porch. When was the last time you saw someone sitting on their front porch? On the front porch individuals could see their neighbors, talk and laugh with those who causally walked by, and survey the front yard as squirrels or other creatures happened by. From your front porch rocking chair you could call out to the neighbor, say hello, and who knows perhaps engage in a small chat. These conversations built community.

Dr. Walter Edgar, foremost South Carolina historian, shared comments at one of the December commencement ceremonies of Newberry College. In that talk he shared visions of the old south and small communities; people knew their neighbors. He concluded that though many would like to return to the "good ole days," such is not the case. He finished his remarks by challenging the graduates to form community wherever they go.

In the work place, in the neighborhood, in the church, wherever you and I go, we have the opportunity to build community, shape a new relationship, and encourage a stranger. In a word we can roll out the red carpet of hospitality.

Now there are some who bring with them a dark cloud and who do anything but warm our hearts and encourage our spirits. Think of the Charlie Brown cartoon with Pigpen. Visually, pigpen was surrounded by a dirty cloud. Some of you know individuals who carry a cloud filled with rain and lightning. The day could be bright and filled with promise, but to them it is going to storm any minute. Truth is they are themselves a storm and their insides are churning.

On the other hand, there are individuals who carry rays of sunshine. Mr. Carl Hamm, a gentleman that I shall always remember, greeted me at every worship service with a smile. He said, "Pastor, It's a beautiful day!" It could be raining outside, a dark and dreary cloud hanging over, but for Carl it was always a beautiful day. His warmth and cheer was contagious.

Christians are called to a contagious spirit of hospitality. Henri Nouwen wrote, "In our world full of strangers, estranged from their own past, culture and country, from their neighbors, friends and family, from their deepest self and their God, we witness a painful search for a hospitable place where life can be lived without fear and where community can be found." Nouwen argues that it is obligatory for Christians to "offer an open and hospitable space where strangers can cast off strangeness and become our fellow human beings."[8] Being nice, warm, friendly, kind and compassionate is not optional. Carrying a ray of sunshine wherever you go is what you and I are called to do.

Hospitality begins with our hearts, our minds, our wills, and our souls before God. We need healing from the inside out. And the only one who can heal us of our hurts and move us to a deep and profound spiritual hospitality is Jesus—the Messiah.

A leper came to Jesus begging him, and kneeling before him said, "If you choose, you can make me clean." Keep in mind that in accordance with established Levitical law codes the leper was considered unclean and was not to associate with others. They were banned to isolation most of their life. Leviticus Chapter 13 verse 45 gives great detail about this disease and how it is to be handled. The leper is instructed that he or she "shall wear torn clothes and let the hair of his head hang loose, and he shall cover his upper lip and cry, Unclean, unclean."

While there is no doubt the man wants to be healed of this dreaded skin disease, do you not think that he wanted far more a restoration to human contact? What does Jesus do? "Moved with pity, Jesus stretched out his hand and touched him." Jesus touched a man with leprosy. Now do you understand how significant this is? The law states, "he is unclean; he shall dwell alone in a habitation outside the camp." In other words, he is to be alone and away from human contact. Jesus touches him and heals him of leprosy.

But, there is more. Jesus charges him to fulfill the law by showing himself to the priest in order to observe the ritual purification laws. Then, Jesus charges him sternly, "Do not say anything to anyone about what has happened here."

Many explanations have been offered for this charge to be quiet. Most scholars have called this the "messianic secret of Mark." The text gives this explanation, "Jesus could no longer go into a town openly." Suffice it to say, practically speaking, Jesus did not want to be known solely as a miracle worker. He was/is the Messiah. This means much more than merely one who can heal.

After he is healed, note what this man does, "But he went out and began to proclaim it freely, and to spread the word." The healed leper was rejoicing in the miracle of Jesus and his restoration to community. He could be with people. He was no longer condemned to isolation, but was free to roam in and about the town. He was like a kid who has been released from a two hour time out. He bounces about and runs to and fro. His happiness and joy is impossible to contain.

The touch of Jesus can transform you. One person at a time, God can remake and refashion his believers into instruments of healing love. We are God's people. Believers are to offer places of holy hospitality. Jesus' touch is meant to warm our hearts for overflowing holy hospitality. You, with Jesus, can create a space and place of love and forgiveness where all can feel welcomed. There are no two people that Jesus cannot bring together in a place of holy hospitality. Strangers become friends through the touch and love of Jesus Christ.

Consider this bizarre example of "hospitality" from the animal kingdom. Aochan is a four foot rat snake at Tokyo's Mutsugoro Okoku Zoo. The rat snake was getting finicky about his food and refused to eat his steady diet of frozen mice. Zookeepers decided to give him a special treat, a live dwarf hamster. The rat snake, Aochan, refused to eat the rodent. And, worst of all, it appears that the snake made friends with the hamster. For some time, the two shared a cage and in the words of the zoo officials, "they play together nicely." So the zoo officials named the hamster Gohan which in Japanese means meal. "I've never seen anything like it," said zookeeper Kazuya Yamamoto. He continued, "Aochan (the snake) seems to enjoy Gohan's company very much. Gohan sometimes even climbs onto Aochan to take a nap on his back."

Imagine, a rat snake befriending a hamster. Now that is bizarre. But it is no more bizarre, really, than the power of Jesus Christ to create a place of hospitality. All around the world Jesus brings his people together for worship. Each Sunday, people worship together who are rich and poor, Democrat and Republican, married and divorced, confident and not so confident, faithful and doubting, secure and seeking. People from every imaginable background are welcomed in order that they might hear God's Word and be healed and transformed.

The touch of Jesus Christ can heal and transform your life. In God's Church strangers become friends and normal space becomes a place of holy hospitality.

Day Thirteen
The Midas Touch

Reading: Psalm 1

Would you like to have the Midas touch? The first answer to that question is, yes. Any one of us would like to think that anything we touch would turn to gold. Midas, you well remember, was the story of the King of Phrygia in Greek Mythology who requested that everything he touched be turned to gold. His request was granted by Dionysius. You know that the story, however, had a sad twist. It seems that all of King Midas's food and water also turned to gold.

I would like for you to entertain the notion that you do in fact have the Midas touch. No, I do not mean to suggest that everything you touch will turn to gold. You know that is not true. But listen well to Psalm 1:3, "They are like trees planted by streams of water, which yield their fruit in its season, and their leaves do not wither. In all that they do, they prosper."

This is a bold statement suggesting that the one who trusts in God is one who will prosper in all he or she does. Now, at face value many of us question such a statement. That is because the age old question rears its ugly head, why do the wicked prosper? Even a review of the scriptures reveals this question in Jeremiah 12:1, "You are always righteous, O LORD, when I bring a case before you. Yet I would speak with you about your justice: Why does the way of the wicked prosper? Why do all the faithless live at ease?"

It often seems that those who prosper the most in our world are those who cheat and lie, but we know that this is not always the case. So what do we make of this statement?

Those who trust in God are like a tree planted by streams of water. We yield fruit and our leaves do not wither. We prosper. Why? How? Well certainly not all of us can turn what we touch into gold. Nor can we say that we will all have excellent health and live to be one hundred years of age.

We do have the promise, however, that we will be nourished. Like the image of the watered tree; we too will be nourished. We will have the food that helps us live through whatever may come our way. Truly, this means whatever.

In all my years of ordained ministry I have seen people survive unbelievable situations. I remember visiting a man in a hospital who had lost most of his face. A tragic car accident had seriously injured everyone in his family. He, however, had borne the worst of the injuries. I went to see him fully expecting bitterness and anger. What I encountered was the opposite. He thanked me for visiting and asked for a prayer of thanks that God had kept his family and him safe. How could this be I wondered? Was this man for real?

"They are like trees planted by streams of water." In all the heartache and all the hurt, people survive. People who trust in God survive. Those who believe that God will provide nourishment for their soul not only survive but thrive. Yes, they even prosper. These are the wounded healers. They bring healing and strength to others simply because they have endured. Look around you. All of us are broken and fragile. Did you ever stop to reflect on the friends you have that have endured hurt and walked through much pain? Many people have faced diseases, life threatening surgeries, deaths and untold other terrible tragedies and yet they survive and many thrive.

Are they for real? Yes, they are. They are the people of God. You can be the person who is like a tree planted by streams of water. You can be strong, not because of your own composition. No! You can be strong when you are planted by the stream of water, living water. You can draw strength from Jesus the living Lord who is living water.

Why do some people make it through dreadful diseases with their hope alive and their love much stronger? Why is it that some people face tragic deaths and then many years later, become instruments of healing for others? Why do some people prosper in faith? They are planted by streams of water, living water, Jesus the Lord. Only in Jesus can people truly prosper.

We do not need the King Midas touch. The real king of Kings, Jesus, touches us with the nourishing sustaining water, the waters of eternal life. He gives the water that strengthens us for living.

Day Fourteen
All is Vanity

Reading: Isaiah 6: 1-6

In my office hangs the strangest of paintings. All who see it are puzzled. Why would a Christian clergyman have a painting of a skull on his wall? From a distance the painting appears to be a skull, but on closer inspection is something quite different. Charles Allen Gilbert painted this optical illusion. Upon closer inspection one can see that it is a woman looking into a mirror while seated at her vanity. The title of the portrait is "All is Vanity!" A clear meaning of this portrait is that vanity, an overemphasis on how one looks, is a failed endeavor, for we will all die and we will become nothing more than a skeleton and ultimately become dust. In essence this painting portrays the human sin of pride. The Catholic Church once enumerated seven deadly sins and one of those was pride.

The book of Proverbs, Chapter 16:18 describes the outcome of pride. "Pride goes before destruction and a haughty spirit before a fall." Pride leads to destruction. The prophet Isaiah was anything but prideful. In fact note how Isaiah Chapter 6, the call narrative of Isaiah, begins. "In the year that King Uzziah died..." Do you find that strange? Or did you pass by that phrase as if it were a fact of little importance? Some of you remember well the date when someone you loved died. You may even relate to a significant spiritual event in your life by the death of another person.

Why not take a serious look at God's call in your life. Now do not immediately think call refers to a Pastor, for God calls all people to various tasks. There is the timely tale of a church that was looking for a new pastor. A retired pastor was temporarily serving as a replacement. One day the retired pastor announced that the bishop would soon be sending the church a new young pastor directly from the seminary. When a little boy heard this announcement, he told his parents that when the new pastor arrived he would no longer be going to Church services. "What are you talking about?" his parents wanted to know. The young boy replied, "When they get priests direct from the cemetery, I'm staying home."

The call of God is illustrated very clearly for us in Isaiah Chapter 6. Here, Isaiah begins the narrative saying, "In the year that King Uzziah died!" Is there more to this than meets the eye? There most certainly is. We start by finding out who is King Uzziah by reading 2 Chronicles 26:16. "But after Uzziah became powerful, his pride led to his downfall." What is most interesting is that when Uzziah died his epitaph said that he was a leper.

Pride led to his downfall. Isaiah communicates by contrast. Isaiah says, "Woe is me, for I am lost; for I am a man of unclean lips, and I dwell in the midst of a people of unclean lips; for my eyes have seen the King, the Lord of Hosts!"

When God calls, he reveals to you your true self. We see that we are broken and flawed people in desperate need of the touch of God's cleansing power. Isaiah understands that he is a sinner. In the same way, you and I are sinners. We are flawed. Our DNA is so wired that we disobey God when left to our own selves. We are no better than those who came before us. There is no evolution of human kindness. There is no progression of humankind getting better and less sinful. Evil is and always has lurked immediately around the corner seeking someone to devour. Sin is real.

Sadly there are people that talk so much about the gospel of love that they exclude the law. Let me explain. Some say Jesus loves us so much that he does not care what we do because we are sinners anyway! Hopefully, you notice the flaw in this logic. We are in need of a cleansing, just as Isaiah needed purging with the burning coal from the altar of God. We need to fall on our knees in humility, fall before the throne of God in obedience, and fall before the cross of Jesus in thanksgiving that we are children of God by the Grace of God! Jesus says, "I am the vine; you are the branches. If a man remains in me and I in him, he will bear much fruit; apart from me you can do nothing." (John 15:5)

Apart from Jesus Christ you and I can do nothing. I really am not interested in what high energy motivational speakers tell you. The scripture is clear. The path to an abundant and fulfilling life is in Christ and apart from Christ you and I are nothing. Humility is the characteristic that understands who we are in relation to one another and who we are in relation to God. With Christ in us we are precious in the eyes of God.

Like Isaiah, God can call you. In 1983 John Sculley, then the 38-year-old President of Pepsi-Cola, was recruited by Steve Jobs, founder of Apple Computer. Jobs issued a tremendous challenge to Sculley. He asked: "Do you want to spend the rest of your life selling sugared water or do you want a chance to change the world?"⁹ What about you? Do you believe that God can call you to change your life? The world?

God's call to you may not be as dramatic as Isaiah's but, nonetheless, consider what that call might mean. All who believe and trust Jesus are called to serve, called to worship, called to love self and neighbor, and called to open their eyes to see the King! You are called to be a witness to Jesus Christ and change the world. It is the power of the Holy Spirit that will enable you to say, "Here I am Lord, send me!"

Day Fifteen
A Time for
Change

Reading: Luke 2:9-11

Every Sunday morning churches gather for worship and the minister delivers announcements. Once in history an announcement was delivered that was the most important pronouncement of all time. It is; "Then an angel of the Lord stood before them, and the glory of the Lord shone around them, and they were terrified. But the angel said to them, "Do not be afraid; for see I am bringing you good news of great joy for all the people: to you is born this day in the city of David a Savior, who is the Messiah, the Lord." (Luke 2:9-11)

This is similar to all other announcements in that it communicates an event. This proclamation, however, differs from all others in a very fundamental way. This declaration communicates the beginning of a new time, a new era in history, and a new beginning. For the birth of this child will change not only the very course of history, but the lives of people everywhere. All things will be new. Luke's detailed account is intended to communicate to us what this new time will look like.

Look at the details. Over the years the beauty of this story has endeared itself to our hearts and we know it by memory but what does it mean? What new time in history is communicated by this intricately detailed story? Basically, how is it that all things will be made new?

It is significant to note that the angels deliver their word to shepherds. These shepherds are living in the field. I know from my own backpacking experience that living out in the field for several days at a time causes the human body to take on a pungent odor. The shepherds probably smelled like their animals. They were not people of culture.

Then, the announcement comes, "You will find a baby wrapped in cloths and lying in a manger." A manger, you got to be kidding! Why not a nicely adorned brass bed, or a throne of some sort? A manger is a feeding trough for animals. A feeding trough is not a pleasant place to nestle a baby. My Great Uncle raised pigs and I remember well the troughs he used to feed his pigs. Certainly not the kind of place I would have snuggled my children.

Contrast this, if you will, with the opening words of Luke 2, "In those days a decree went out from Caesar Augustus." He was given the name Augustus by the Roman Senate in 27 BC. This Caesar is the one who is credited with bringing great peace, prosperity and cultural achievements to the Roman Empire. The time of his reign came to be called the Augustan Age. Even the name by which he is called "Augustus" means "exalted."

This exalted ruler no doubt placed his head on a feather pillow and slept on the finest of silken sheets. And yet in stark contrast, Luke tells us of another exalted one; one who was born in the feeding trough. His birth was announced to lowly smelly shepherds. We have become so comfortable with this quaint, cute story that we have whitewashed all the simplicity and messiness right out of it. Luke wants us to see the stark and striking contrast. What does this mean? How is it that this plain birth in a feeding trough announced to smelly shepherds can make all things new?

God comes in the lowly, humble form of a baby to illustrate his servant nature. This was illustrated when Jesus spoke shocking words to his disciples, "For even the Son of Man did not come to be served, but to serve, and to give his life as a ransom for many." (Mark 10:45) The nature of Jesus Christ is not a kingly power that controls, but a gentle love that cares.

God makes all things new in Jesus Christ by being one of us. By identifying with the oppressed and the humble, the lowly and despised, the hungry and the homeless, God shows that Jesus Christ is a Savior for all people. God's love and care in Christ is for all people. Not only the religious, not only the saints, not only the cultured, but Jesus was born for every man, woman and child in this world.

Often it is our pretensions to be "good" that interfere with God's salvation work in us. How can we be healed or how can we be redeemed or how can Jesus change our hearts and make us new, when we think to ourselves that we have it all together? Luke paints this vivid scene of Jesus birth to ultimately point us to Jesus as a suffering servant and then finally to point us to the cross.

This means that we do not climb a ladder of good deeds to God, but rather that God comes to us. We can never make ourselves good enough for God. God does not notice us because we are noticeable. God in Christ comes to us because it is the nature, the very essence of God to love and to serve.

The angels announce, "For unto you is born this day!" The word points us to something more than the hands on a clock, but to the changing of all history. This day is for you. Jesus was born for a purpose. Jesus was born so that you might be loved and served by him. May Jesus serve you by opening your heart so that the Love of God might pour into your life in an overwhelming and abundant way! May Jesus serve you by making your life fresh, new and invigorating! May Jesus serve you by giving you the ability to sing with the depths of your soul, "Glory to God in the highest and peace to all people on earth!"

Day Sixteen
The Black Death

Reading: Romans 5:12-19

Picture yourself in the year 1350. You are in Europe and all around you friends, neighbors, and relatives are becoming ill, and many if not most, are dying. The symptoms you see are similar to the flu. There is headache, nausea, vomiting, aching joints, and a general feeling of ill health. People are living in fear. The Black Death it came to be called. Why? Because in the few hours before death the bubonic plague would cause respiratory failure and the body would turn a purple color. The sickness spread throughout Europe and China. What began as a bite from a flea spread to humans and spread rapidly.

Thousands upon thousands of years ago, one man brought a disease into our midst. His name was Adam, the first human being. This was the spiritual plague to end all plagues. It is this illness that can destroy not only the body, yes, even the body, but also the soul—the very essence of what it means to be a human being. Through Adam came sin. Through the act of Adam's disobedience came separation from the Creator and separation from one another. Self -centered behavior and narcissism became the core of our being. Deny it if you will, but to do so is to ignore the very basic truth of the scripture and the very reality that we see around us.

And it is through sin that death came, death—real death, a decaying body, a broken soul, a life less than what it could become. This destruction called death spread to all because all have sinned. This is truly the only real Black Death. And all of us are infected with this original sin. All of us choose to disobey God day after day. Death was and is the destroyer; death had dominion from Adam to Moses. Death was the victor.

Why, you ask, am I affected by this one man's disobedience? It is because you and I are atypical humans. We are human beings and it is our nature and even our very choice to do as we please. We want to be captains of our own destiny, lights for our own paths, and judges in our own parade. We are sinners. We are sick and whether we want to hear it or not it is the truth.

Put any of us in a perfect place. Big house, nice cars, all of the material possessions you could ever need and want and then let someone tell us that we cannot do one thing and that is the one thing we will want to do. Do not eat this fruit Adam—that is all God asked. You know what happened? What followed is the scourge of humanity.

One man's disobedience, one man's failure, one man and woman brought this to us all and so here we are. Broken people sick with sin. It is not only the things we do that are sin; it is the separation from God. How many of us have the relationship with God that is close and intimate at all times and in all places as it should be? This is the legacy left to you and me by Adam and Eve. We can never fully approach the holy God completely on our own.

The Apostle Paul tells us that one man's disobedience led to one man's obedience. Through the obedience of Jesus Christ, the many will be made righteous. Jesus literally became purple, suffered the Black Death, and cried out in anguish and pain, "My God, my God, why have you forsaken me?" Feeling the pain of separation, feeling the pain of death, feeling the pain of sin—your sin, and your negligence of him as the one and only Lord, it was you and I who drove those nails. It was I, yes I, who ran and hid as did Peter.

Oh pitiful lot that we are, who will deliver us from this body of death? Jesus will. Jesus was obedient to death and in death. Jesus embraced the plague of humanity and took it upon his own shoulders. I should have died, but Jesus died for me, in my place, because of my sins. Jesus was and is the perfect lamb, the sacrifice. Jesus is the obedient one and through him we have the free gift, the abundance of grace.

Baptism is our vaccine. Baptism joins us to the death and resurrection of our Lord and Savior Jesus Christ. Paul writes in Romans 6:3-5, "Do you not know that all of us who have been baptized into Christ Jesus were baptized into his death? Therefore we have been buried with him by baptism into death, so that, just as Christ was raised from the dead by the glory of the Father, so we too might walk in newness of life. For if we have been united with him in a death like his, we will certainly be united with him in a resurrection like his."

A Columbia, SC congregation placed a sign out front near its cross with these words, "Is it nothing to you, all you who pass by?" I ask you today, can you and I possibly be locked into our old painful and broken ways, or shall we be changed? Will you pray for the Messiah to pour his grace into your sinful human heart and bring you everlasting healing?

Day Seventeen
Chicken or Fox

Reading: Luke 13:31-35

Why did the chicken cross the road? To get to the other side, right? How about, why did the chicken cross the road? He crossed to show the possum how. How about one more? Why did the chicken cross the road? He crossed in order to escape from the fox. I admit this one is not too funny and I would not be invited to any stand- up comedy clubs with a joke like that. However, that is the point, it isn't a joke. These are the images from Luke's gospel.

Look at it closely. First, there is King Herod. This king Herod is Herod of Antipas who ruled from 4 BC to 39 AD. He is the Herod who had John the Baptist beheaded. He is also the Herod who married his half brother's wife. One scholar reports that this Herod is "idle, vicious and extravagant."[10] This is also the same Herod before whom Jesus appeared. It is this Herod that Jesus calls a fox.

So, the first image we have is of a King described as vicious by scholars and called a fox by Jesus. Now, please fast-forward to the latter part of this text for our second image, that of a chicken. Jesus says of his children, "How often have I desired to gather your children together as a hen gathers her brood under her wings, and you were not willing!"

Now, I ask you, which would you prefer to be in this text, the fox or the chicken? Hmm! I know a little bit about chickens. I had two white roosters growing up and they were pretty fierce. They chased away the letter carrier and so we had to give them to my grandfather who lived in the country. But truly, in a face off with a fox, they would lose. But a mother hen, well, she would squawk and make all sorts of noises and probably cover the little ones with her wings. In the final battle, the mother hen would lose and be eaten by the fox.

Why, I ask you, is this text filled with the presence of these two images? There is King Herod who represents great worldly power. This is the King Herod who is a vicious and extravagant man. He probably had anything and everything he wanted. This is Herod the fox, wise and cunning. Then there is Jesus, like the mother hen, who is squawking and not too bright. Hmm! What is going on here?

Could it be that the chicken really wins after all? Could it be that the chicken does something significant in the battle with the powers of the world? I believe these images to be quite intentional. Jesus uses the images to contrast the power of the world, cunning and crafty, with the power of the word, safe and sacrificial. True safety, true protection, and true shelter reside under the wings of the chicken because the chicken will give her life for the protection of her little ones.

Jesus demonstrates to the powers of the world that he will not be distracted from his mission to die. His face is set toward Jerusalem. Jesus is going to Jerusalem no matter what the Herod's of the world say. It does not matter about the reputation of Jerusalem, a place where prophets are killed. It does not matter that it may appear to the world that chickens always lose to foxes. It is not so with Jesus.

Jesus dies in order for us to live. Jesus gives the ultimate sacrifice, his life. This is the good news. It is this news that invites a response. One cannot look upon the cross, really see it, really observe it, really and truly behold the dying, loving, Jesus, and not be moved. This is where you and I fit in the story. What will we be? Will we be a chicken or a fox? If foxes represent worldly wisdom and chickens represent the wisdom of the word, then you and I should choose to be chickens. I know it doesn't sound so inviting, Chickens for Jesus, does it? What does this mean for us?

If indeed Jesus did give the ultimate sacrifice for us, are we not in turn compelled to live a sacrificial life? There is a lot of cheap grace circulating these days. There is a lot of "do nothing" Christianity. There is a lot of commitment to buildings and committees and programs, but what about love for Jesus. Jesus gives sacrificial love. In response to the great gift Jesus has given, will you commit to Jesus?

Day Eighteen
Are you Smelling the Aroma or Tasting the Bread?

Reading: John 3:14-21

Flower's industry was a bakery in Spartanburg, South Carolina. It was located on the Hearon Circle. I passed this spot regularly to visit my grandparents. Interestingly enough, one could not pass by without the enticing aroma of baked goods. Maybe it was an advertising trick or something, but it is sufficient to say that passing the bakery almost always invoked the desire for a fresh pastry. Is it possible to smell the aroma of a bakery and never taste the bread?

Think about that question a moment. Would anyone look at a box of rich chocolates and never taste one? I realize some of you are on a diet and chocolates and bread are off limits and my analogy is lost on you!

Jesus said in John's gospel, "I am the living bread that came down from heaven." I contend that far too many Christians think that they have arrived on their faith journey. They got baptized; were catechized and confirmed. In some traditions they may have even submitted to being "sanctified." These Christians have even served on a few committees and done a few good deeds. It is, however, evident that their spiritual journey stopped somewhere along the way. Bibles are gathering dust and prayer time is filled with the images of a 13-inch cathode ray tube better known as a television.

In other words they smell the aroma, but do not taste the bread! They may appear to participate on the surface, but are not hungering and thirsting for the righteousness that only Jesus Christ can give. Acts 4:12 reads, "And there is salvation in no one else, for there is no other name under heaven given among men by which we must be saved."

John 3:16 is most familiar to all of us. This text, however, does not indicate that God loves the world so much that all those who pay lip service are saved. This is not about saying the right things. To bear the name of Christ means more than saying polite and nice words each day. This text is not about thinking the right things. If belief were about knowledge, then it would be nothing short of what the early church fathers called Gnosticism. Gnosticism was an early heresy that purported that supernatural knowledge given by divine revelation was the channel for salvation.

John 3:14-21 is about believing, and believing is following and following means living the faith day in and day out. It is living the faith when there is great joy and when there is sadness. It is being faithful when we are blessed with an abundance of wealth and when we face poverty. Believing is coming to the light. Coming to the light means doing those things that bring joy to God's heart. Believing takes our minds, our hearts, our strength, and our souls. Salvation affects are intellect, our emotions, our will and our spirits.

Coming to believe in Jesus, truly believe, is rarely a 10 minute conversion experience. God can do anything and perform any miracle including bringing people to faith and belief in the blink of an eye, but the human will and intellect are often resistant. It takes time for an individual to grow in faith. God gives faith in the miracle of baptism. God gives faith and strengthens faith in the miracle of his body and blood served in, with, and under the bread and wine of Holy Communion. God gives faith in the mere hearing of the word, but growth in belief takes time. To suggest that one can say one prayer, make one decision, and then be a believer, shortchanges deep, life changing salvation.

Think of coming to believe as a process. Some have suggested that people move from scoffer to skeptic, from skeptic to curious, from curious to seeker and from seeker to believer; and perhaps there are miniature steps in between these. Even long term believers have moments of clarity and faith mixed with days of doubt. Ask yourself, where are you in your belief in Jesus? Do you merely smell the aroma of salvation, or do you taste the living bread?

Luke records that from the sixth hour until the ninth hour on Good Friday darkness was over the whole land. Condemnation and darkness came to earth that Friday afternoon as the only Son of God died the death of a criminal. His crime was bearing your sins. His punishment was your doubts and disbelief. His death was real. His resurrection was real. I can believe in this God and so can you. Pray for the Holy Spirit to give you growth in belief.

Day Nineteen
The Sin Virus

Reading: Romans 5: 17-21

Here is a definition from "Tabers Cyclopedic Medical Dictionary," "A pathogen made of nucleic acid inside a protein shell, which can grow and reproduce only after infecting a host cell." This is the definition of a virus. Viruses need a host cell and after inhabiting the host cell will often destroy it. Viruses thrive by spreading to other cells. In a science fiction movie made popular several years ago entitled the Matrix, Agent Smith, as he was called, said to another actor, "Humans are like viruses they spread and devour what is around them and then move on."

Well we are not viruses and it was only a movie, but the quotation stuck in my mind. Why? It is because our behavior, our actions, and our thoughts, are often like a virus. That is to say our bad behaviors, actions, and thoughts spread and cause much damage. Paul writes, "Just as sin came into the world through one man, and death came through sin, and so death spread to all because all have sinned..." It all began quite innocently. It was a perfect paradise, a garden of all the needed nutrients, and an opportunity to walk and talk with God. What could be more perfect? And yet the action of one person, disobedience, led to disobedience of all. Death also spread to all. Sin is like a virus. It infects the host. It infects you and me and begins the breakdown and we become sick. The sin virus affects all people and no one is immune.

The entire Old Testament is a story of God's intervention with the people of God. From the very beginning we see the effects of the spread of sin, from the murder of Abel to the eventual flood of the earth. Even after God began his covenant relationship with Abraham, the influence of sin continued. Let's not kid ourselves, sin is a pervasive influence. The force of evil is alive and well in our culture.

One church council reported watching a video series on evangelism at its annual retreat. The well-informed and well -intentioned pastor said that we should not begin our services of worship reminding people of sin. This presenter's contention is that people seeking God do not need to hear first and foremost about sin and their need to ask for forgiveness. This sounds rather inviting. It is, however, dishonest and unrealistic. Do you and I not know that we are broken people and do we not know that this sin virus eats at us every day? We have all felt its effects. We catch fever; you know the fever to have more than we need. We might call it envy and jealousy fever, but whatever we call it we know it is real.

Doctors know that there are 400 known viruses. While Christians know that there may be thousands upon thousands of individual sins, there is only one sickness and that is separation from God. Sin separates us from a right relationship with God, but wait. Don't give up because all is not lost.

You see the Apostle Paul continued with these words, "Therefore just as one man's trespass led to condemnation for all, so one man's act of righteousness leads to justification and life for all." There is the remedy; the antivirus, if you will. There is one man who broke the spread. There is one man who was unaffected. There is one man who stopped it all, once and for all. His name is Jesus. His act of righteousness was our salvation. His act of obedience brought us life. His suffering enabled us to have healing. As Paul writes, "So by the one man's obedience the many will be made righteous." The power of Christ extends to all.

The remedy for the disease is a relationship with Jesus Christ. Christ boosts the immune system, fights the fevers of the world, and kills the invading disease of sin, day by day. You and I are called to go forth and inoculate the whole world with this powerful serum of life. Because even though sin can spread like wildfire, even more so can God's love and forgiveness.

The power of Christ and his message can change the world, one person at a time. Out of response to his unconditional grace, his love and forgiveness, we can do no other than live our lives in joyful obedience. And who knows you may influence someone whom God will use to affect one other, or ten others, or maybe even millions! God can spread the power of his glorious grace using you!

In May of 1934 a Charlotte, North Carolina farmer lent a pasture to some thirty local businessmen who wanted to devote a day of prayer for Charlotte because the Depression had spread spiritual apathy in the city. They had planned, despite the indifference of the ministerial association, to hold an evangelistic campaign later that year. During that day of prayer on the land their leader, Vernon Patterson, prayed, "Out of Charlotte the Lord would raise up someone to preach the Gospel to the ends of the earth." The businessmen next erected in the city a large "tabernacle" of raw pine on a steel frame, where for eleven weeks from September 1934 a renowned, fiery Southern evangelist named Mordecai Fowler Ham, and his song leader, Walter Ramsay, shattered the complacency of church-going Charlotte. Well, God did hear their prayer. The farmer who lent his pasture for the prayer meeting was Franklin Graham and his son Billy listened to the message of Jesus and the rest is history. He preached it and we know it. Jesus is our cure.

Day Twenty
On the Fringe

Reading: John 20:19-31

Dr. Martin Saarinen, professor emeritus of Lutheran Theological Southern Seminary, led student retreats. In 1985, our last year together as a seminary class, Marty invited us to participate in a most interesting assignment. He divided the room into huge concentric circles. Those of us who felt like we really belonged were to stand in the innermost circle. As the circles progressed outward we were to stand where we symbolically felt we belonged to the class. Slowly, we each moved to a spot. I was a class officer and felt really close to a number of folks in the class so I stood near the center. I watched as other classmates of mine moved toward the center and others further and further out. There on the outside ring stood Mike. I was shocked and so were others. He felt on the fringe.

Have you ever felt on the fringe? Have you ever felt as though you were not in the loop of things as though you did not belong? How easily it is to get lost in the shuffle, especially in a large crowd of people. For instance, what would happen if you were to draw a group of concentric circles with your family and friends? And suppose I asked you to place yourself in the inner circle if you felt as though you really belonged, the next circle if you sort of felt that closeness, and then in the outer circle if you did not feel close at all. Where would you be? Sadly, some of you would place yourself in the outer circle.

What if we changed the criteria from your sense of belonging to your sense of faith? In the center you would say, "I have a strong and confident faith in Jesus as my Lord." And then on outward to the outermost circle where you would say, "I am often plagued with doubt and am not sure what I believe." In that doubting circle you would have the company of none other than Thomas of biblical fame. Yes, it is doubting Thomas, the one who insisted that he would not believe unless he saw with his own two eyes. Thomas was on the fringe!

What do you think is Jesus response to people on the fringe? Does Jesus castigate them for their lack of faith? Certainly, at one point in Jesus ministry we hear his weariness as he says, "O faithless and perverse generation, how long am I to be with you? How long am I to bear with you? Bring him here to me." (Matthew 17:17) Far more often, however, we see examples that clearly show us Jesus concern for the fringe. Jesus will go to the outermost extremes to bring someone to faith and to help them in their belief. Jesus said to Thomas, "Put your finger here and see my hands. Reach out your hand and put it in my side. Do not doubt but believe."

Many people struggle with doubts and even feel the depths of despair. You may even feel on the fringe currently. Jesus has a word for you; do not doubt but believe. To believe is a great gift. To believe in Jesus is to persist in our faith even in the face of conflict, even in the face of hurt, even in the face of pain, and even in the face of death. But even though Jesus will go to great lengths to bring us to belief and even keep us in the faith, we have a responsibility for our growth in faith.

A friend of mine likes to share about all the great opportunities and experiences he has had. He began a career as a crop-duster and ended up as a stunt pilot doing air shows all over the United States. Many of his great experiences, he says, are merely because he showed up. He even wrote and published a book with one chapter entitled, Just show up! Get in the game he says.

Our growth in faith often means little more than showing up. If we hear the word read and preached and participate in a Christian community, we are doing our part to show up and allow God to give us growth. The apostle Paul wrote, "But how are men to call upon him in whom they have not believed? And how are they to believe in him of whom they have never heard? And how are they to hear without a preacher?" (Romans 10:14) How are we to believe and how are we to stay out of the fringe unless we show up.

Thomas was there with the disciples when he needed to be there and Jesus showed up for him. Jesus brought him from doubt to faith. Jesus does the same for us every time we hear his word and share in his supper.

A multinational corporation hires in a most unique way. Applicants for managerial jobs are seated in an area outside the office of the interviewing Vice President. Nearby is the Vice President's secretary. As usual, her tasks are many and varied such as filing, answering the phone repeatedly, typing a letter, and even being asked to take something to someone else's office.

The managerial applicants are all eyewitnesses to the busy secretary. At one point in her frantic pace the secretary asks the waiting managerial applicant to pick up a file and take it to an office across the hall. The applicants normally respond in three ways. Most refuse to be drafted into manual labor. A few will reluctantly get up and offer to watch the phone, but insist that they want to keep one eye on the Vice President's door. Rarely, one individual will pick up the file and deliver it to the office across the hall. Guess who waits for them! Upon delivering the file, they are greeted by the Vice President for Personnel who informs the applicant that he or she made it to the final round of applicants simply because he or she was willing to serve.

Our Lord Jesus wants to serve you a huge helping of faith. But we need to get in the game, participate in the fellowship of other Christians, worship regularly, read the scripture, pray without ceasing and show up.

Day Twenty One
How do we know anything?

Reading: John 17: 1-11

How do you know anything? For instance, if you were interested in learning more about Tarantula spiders, how would you find out? Once while watching the program Animal Planet I learned new insights about these gargantuan spiders and their habits. One of my Sunday school teachers use to say, if there is something you do not know, look it up. My college philosophy professor said something a bit similar, "my job is to teach you to think!" That is the key. It is to think and to know about our world around us.

How do you know anything? Do you look things up? Reflect for a moment about knowing God. Jesus says it succinctly, "And this is eternal life, that they know thee the only true God, and Jesus Christ whom thou hast sent." To know God is to know Jesus and to know Jesus is to have eternal life. Jesus says, "Truly, truly, I say to you, he who hears my word and believes him who sent me, has eternal life; he does not come into judgment, but has passed from death to life." (John 5:24)

Knowing Jesus means eternity living. Eternity living is more than a hope for heaven, but is a life lived now in the hope of heaven, and life lived now that gives honor and glory to God. Eternity living is living each day and every moment in the presence of God. Eternity living is to live and know that each day and each moment is a time to practice living forever with one another. If you are going to live forever, then now is the time to practice your love for others. There really is no place for procrastination.

How do you know Jesus? Certainly the journey of knowledge begins with reading, studying, and praying for the enlightenment of the Holy Spirit. Too many individuals profess faith in Christ, but know little about his word. Knowing Jesus begins with knowing the Holy Scripture.

When we read the gospel in many of our churches we stand. Why do we stand? We stand to honor Christ. In the fourth century St. Augustine said, "When we read the gospel it is as if Jesus was standing in our midst." When we read the gospel it is as if Jesus is standing among us and speaking to us, thus we stand in honor of Jesus and his word. To know Jesus is to know his word.

I once knew an engineer who decided to take up golf after his retirement. He had never played before and knew nothing about the game. Typical of an analytical person, he secured a few books and videos to learn all about golf. So, he knew golf. But as you might surmise there is more than knowing the game is there not? He then played golf. He invited me to join him and I did until the day he began to play well. He began to score in the mid to high 80's and my score, let's say I am still trying to know golf.

You begin to know Jesus by knowing his word, but knowing implies more than book knowledge. The words of God are meant not only to infiltrate our minds, but inculcate our lives. We have to play the faith, play it out day in and day out. We need to have constant conversation with God our maker. We need to experience God. And how do we do that? For some it is a quiet moment on a mountain top. Others experience God as they watch a cardinal alight on a bird feeder outside the window. Some experience God in the warm embrace of a caring Christian friend. On a retreat, around the dinner table, listening to music, and at the side of a dying friend, these are but a few of the places that we can experience the presence of God. All of us experience God in a variety of places and often in our place of worship.

John Wesley, the founder of Methodism, was reading Martin Luther's commentary on Romans when he felt his heart strangely warmed. A feeling of warmth overcame this man and his life took on more meaning for the kingdom of God. But make no mistake, an experience of God can never and should never be apart from the knowledge of the Word of God. There are far too many heresies proliferating under the umbrella of being "Christian." Too many individuals say, "I believe this or I believe that," without first consulting the Holy Scripture.

Sadly, many of our denominations are confronting great evils. These controversies even make their way into late night television jokes. For instance on one night Jay Leno commented that the church was seeking to write a policy or guidebook that defined proper sexual conduct. Upon which Leno joked, you have a book; it is called the Bible. I am sure many laughed, but think of the profundity of that joke.

There were three phrases that marked the Reformation begun by Martin Luther. They are scripture alone, faith alone, and grace alone. To know Jesus is to know his word. Through scripture alone we have our guidebook for faithful and eternity living. Through faith alone we know Jesus in a relationship that truly is personal and communal. Through grace alone we stand before God worthy to enter into paradise.

To know God is to Know Jesus and to know Jesus is to know his word and to experience Jesus in daily eternity living. Begin today fresh and anew with Jesus in your life.

Day Twenty Two
Where is Waldo?

Reading: John 20: 1-18

Where is Waldo? This was the craze in books some years ago. A quick look at this book reveals the confusion one encounters in trying to find the hidden figure. One would think that we are playing a similar game of hide and seek with the deposed tyrants of the world. For instance many people asked the haunting question, where was Osama Bin Laden and where was Saddam Hussein? Both of whom are now dead. With a bounty on their head and armies in search of them; it did not seem realistic that they could elude the military for so long. A person gets the impression from an initial reading of the twentieth chapter of the gospel of John that the title might be, "Where is Jesus?"

That is certainly the question on the minds of the disciples. First, we see Mary Magdalene in this story. Mary Magdalene went to the tomb early on Sunday morning to anoint the body of Jesus. Her trip, however, turns into a search mission. The body of Jesus was not in the tomb. And so she exclaims, "They have taken the Lord out of the tomb, and we do not know where they have laid him."

A reading of these first eight verses of chapter 20 gives the impression that the search and rescue mission had gone awry. Peter came out with the other disciple. The other disciple gets there first and looks in the tomb. Then Peter arrives and he looks in the tomb. Meanwhile Mary is standing outside weeping and still searching, "They have taken away my Lord and I do not know where they have laid him."

Where is Jesus? This is an old question. Many have addressed this inquiry. Renowned scholar Albert Schweitzer published a book entitled, "In Search of the Historical Jesus." His hope was to get at what he thought to be the real Jesus. Today, there are many who purport to do the same. Sadly, many scholars challenge the historicity of the resurrection and in essence frolic in heresy. Mary, however, knows better, for she knew Jesus and spent time with Jesus. For her, Jesus is very real.

So, in her grief Mary looks for Jesus. Strikingly, however, Mary sees Jesus standing at the tomb, but did not know him. She did not recognize him. It is easy to explain why she did not see Jesus when he looked right at her. Mary was looking for Jesus, to be sure, but she was looking for a dead Jesus. She was looking in the tomb for a body. She was looking for a decaying corpse. It is no wonder that her eyes could not perceive the man who stood before her was Jesus. Mary does not find Jesus, but Jesus finds her. Jesus asks why she is weeping. Jesus calls her name and Mary sees Jesus. Mary is found!

Where is Jesus in your life? Are you frantically looking in the wrong places? Are you looking for a Jesus who does not exist? Are you searching for a historical Jesus that fits what you want or need him to be?

Easter is the most historic day of the Christian church. On Easter Sunday churches proclaim most loudly the resurrected Jesus. Jesus is the man who died and rose again from the dead and lives and reigns for all eternity. This is the real Jesus. This is the real story.

Jesus is real. Jesus is alive and he is searching for you. He searches for you in acts of service. He searches for you when you read the scripture. He searches for you when you gather in fellowship with other believers even for something as simple as a meal. He searches for you when you enter into a church for worship. Jesus is present in worship, in the reading of scripture, in fellowship, and in your prayers. Jesus is present and alive, not absent and dead. We do not need to look for Jesus, because Jesus is not lost. The answer to the question, where is Jesus is simply this, Jesus lives in the lives of his followers.

He lives in the believer; and to those who are still searching Jesus keeps calling your name, just as he called the name of Mary. And Jesus will call your name over and over as many times as necessary to get you to see the real Jesus. Jesus is the victor over death, and he wants to call your name. He calls your name when you are facing despair and doubt. He calls your name when you face illness. He calls your name even in death. Listen to his call.

As the children's hymns says so well, "Jesus loves me this I know, for the Bible tells me so, little ones to him belong they are weak but he is strong. Yes Jesus loves me for the Bible tells me so."

Day Twenty Three
Real Death, Great Life

Reading: John 20: 1-18

Some years ago Geoff Smith set out to break the world record for the longest time being buried under the ground. He planned to live in a coffin-shaped box for 180 days. Consider, however, that his living quarters were equipped with a television, lights and restroom facilities. Food and drink were to be provided through a small tube that would connect him with the outside world. My question to this is why?

Is it fame? Is it having your name in the Guinness book? Is it some bizarre fascination with death? Is this a mockery of real death? Or is he numb to real death and what it means. I suspect the latter. Smith and his stunt is only one example of our unrealistic perception of death.

First, we view killing on television and movies as normal. We have all watched as someone dies on television and we might even be yawning as we observe. People are blown up, shot up, thrown off cliffs, and in horror movies the unmentionable happens. Are we numb?

Second, when we visit funeral homes we see corpses that have been decorated by funerary sleight of hand. There are the cosmetics and the fancy lace-filled caskets. We say things like they look good or, "he looks like himself." Now, do not misunderstand, I am not suggesting that our rituals are bad. I merely raise the question, are we doing these things to soften the impact of death or even to negate that death is real.

Third, people persist in promoting the myth of immortality. The popular Greek notion of immortality is based on the assumption that the human body is merely drab clothing for a soul and the soul is the real self. This leads to the belief that the soul is immortal and therefore cannot die. Such thinking negates God as the one who creates life and who can end life. Immortality of the soul ultimately is hope for something lasting rather than something new.[11]

Death is the dead end for us. Joseph Heller in a novel with contemporary, crass language about the reality of death, wrote, "Man is matter...Drop him out a window and he'll fall. Set fire to him and he'll burn. Bury him and he'll rot like other kinds of garbage. The spirit is gone, man is garbage."[12]

Death is death. No thoughts, no feelings, no sensations, and no consciousness will survive. The scriptures call death the last enemy.

Jesus dies. That is the darkness of Good Friday. That is the reality of the crucifixion. That is the pain of the world, and that is the agony he felt when he cried from the cross, "My God, My God why have you forsaken me?" Jesus was placed in a tomb. His limp and lifeless body was wrapped in cloth covered with spices.

And then came Sunday morning. Peter, John, and Mary Magdalene go to the tomb. Mary goes to pay her respects to the body. She is there and anticipates death. She weeps. She is afraid. She cannot even recognize Jesus when he first speaks to her. And she fails miserably to see Jesus. Why? Because something has happened that has never happened before and has not happened since. This is a new thing. This is a cataclysmic event unlike any in the history of time. Jesus entered death and three days later was alive.

Some of you will recall a similar scriptural story about a man named Lazarus. He died and Jesus brought him back to life. But Lazarus died again. His body wore out again and he died again. But with Jesus something radically different takes place; Jesus is transformed. Jesus has a glorified body, as evidenced by his word to Mary at the tomb, "Do not hold on to me, because I have not yet ascended to the Father."

Mary Magdalene goes to the tomb expecting to find death and life finds her. And the life is Jesus. Jesus is life. Jesus is resurrection. As David Buttrick has said, "The resurrection of Jesus Christ is not primarily good news about our chances for survival, a once a year hope of hereafter. Primarily, the resurrection is good news of Jesus Christ."[13] This is a story about God who is so powerful that he can conquer death once and for all. God can conquer death for all people who cling to him in faith for all time, even eternity.

God speaks Mary's name and Mary's faith is activated. She says, "Teacher." God wants to speak your name and awaken your faith so that your name will ring out for eternity. As unbelievable as it seems, this is the central content of Christianity. God gives life. Yes, death is painfully real. Death destroys, but God gives life through his son, eternal life to all who believe. And God will even help you to believe through the power of his Spirit.

A December 1999 article in the New York Times recounted the story of a little boy named Travis. Travis lived in Memphis Tennessee and was known to many in the city. As the story goes, a friend stopped by the East Memphis apartment where Travis and his mother lived. The friend found Travis, a nine-year old boy, living alone with his mother lying dead on the living room floor. The boy said he did not tell anyone about her death because he was afraid of what would happen to him. So he got himself up every morning, made breakfast, went to school, did his homework, and went shopping with money he found around the house. He lived with his dead mother for one month. Imagine someone living with the dead. Is this story not symbolic of so many lives today? Many people go through the motions of life, but are not fully living.

They are not fully living because they have not come to grips with death. Countless people are hurting and hoping for something more. They are living in fear and searching for authentic life.

Christians are called out of death into life. A living Lord calls us by name and asks that we live, live fully and completely. We are to live in anticipation of that day when we die, yes, die. Because when we die in the Lord we are born to eternal life. This is the message of the Messiah for you.

Day Twenty Four
The Outer Limits

Reading: Mark 9:38-39

The Outer Limits was a science fiction television program that pushed the limits of belief. The phrase works well in describing those things or events that you and I find beyond belief. For instance, we might say that something beyond our belief is in the outer limits. What is beyond belief? Well for one there is the idea that there are people doing God's kingdom work who are not in a church. Seriously, is this possible? Consider what the disciples said to Jesus. "Teacher, we saw someone casting out demons in your name, and we tried to stop him, because he was not following us."

Allow me to put this in modern conversation; if someone is not a member of a church they are not do-ing God's kingdom work. Jesus responds to this by say-ing, "Do not stop him; for no one who does a deed of power in my name will be able soon afterward to speak evil of me." God's kingdom work is in the outer limits and I do not mean out there, but rather God's work is large, expansive and beyond our limits, or rather be-yond our limits of understanding. God works with us to bring about his work; and God works with others as well to bring about his work.

One story of the Old Testament that always fascinated me is in Isaiah 45. There you will read that God chose the King of Persia, a man named Cyrus. God calls Cyrus, "The anointed," and yet we are told that, "I summon you by name and bestow on you a title of honor, though you do not acknowledge me." (45:4)

It is hard to belief that God can use someone for his purposes and the person does not even acknowledge God. What does this mean? It means that God will fulfill his purpose with you or without you. Now thankfully, God invites you to participate in his Kingdom work. You can sit by on the sidelines or you can get in the game. Frankly, the choice is pretty clear to me, sitting idly by is not healthy for spiritual growth.

So, though God can and often does bring about his work and his will with us or without us, God's kingdom work is not out of our grasp, it is not beyond our ability. In fact, God's kingdom work is within our grasp. How? "Whoever gives you a cup of water to drink because you bear the name of Christ will by no means lose the reward." Building the Kingdom of God is as simple as giving someone a cup of water. Extending the hand of fellowship, working to encourage another Christian, building a habitat house, visiting a home bound person or nursing center, working quietly behind the scenes to build a house of worship and praying for God to strengthen other congregations also, is kingdom work.

I am amazed at the competitiveness that often emerged between Christians and other congregations. Gaustad, a church historian, recounts in his book, A Documentary History of Religion in America, about a Hugenot minister and Anglican priest exchanging sharp words about a member.

There is no precedent for Christian people attacking one another. All too often Christians behave like Lemmings and yearn for the "Church for the moment." In many places, at least in the United States, congregations become fads. Competition emerges between two, three or even more congregations. Sadly, people move to and fro with the personality of the minister or the expansiveness of the program or the size of the building or because of the make-up of the membership. If the word of God is preached, and two or three are gathered in the name of Jesus, then the Almighty God is present. It is the word of God that determines that a gathering of people is the Church of Jesus Christ. It does not matter if it is the Church in the Wildwood or the First Church of Boston.

God's kingdom work is done by you and me when we yield our will, our wishes, and our wants to the will of God. In other words there are limits; there are boundaries within which we must work. Jesus says plainly, if your hand causes you to stumble cut it off; if your foot causes you to stumble, cut it off, if your eye causes you to stumble, tear it out. This is very strong language, which means if you are divisive in the work of God's kingdom, if you cause a person who is trying to grow in faith to stumble, then woe be unto you.

In fact the consequences are greater for teachers, preachers and Christian leaders. These persons must answer to God. They are accountable for their actions, thoughts, deeds and must not cause a "little one," that is to say someone who is a person of little faith, to stumble. But in reality this applies to all who would follow Jesus. It would be better if a millstone were hung around the neck of someone stunting another's spiritual growth. A millstone is a very large stone. As if that is not enough, God intends that we work in his kingdom, being positive role models and people of faith for all people; and if we are not, there is Hell to pay, literally.

Hell is mentioned three times. It is as if there were a flashing neon sign that says you better pay attention here. And then there is this graphic description, "where there worm never dies and the fire is never quenched." In other words, there is endless destruction. Worms eat decaying carcasses and eventually quit because there is no more flesh left. In hell the worms never die; they eat and eat and eat and the fire burns and burns and burns. This is no pretty picture.

God intends for us to get busy and to do God's work. It is as simple as giving a cup of water to another believer. God sees all the small deeds of kindness done to and for his people, but the reverse is also true. If there are no deeds of kindness and if there is a lukewarm Christianity; it will be dealt with severely.

You can choose to ignore God's promptings. You can choose to look away from the needs God sends to you. You can choose to tear down the people of God or ignore the needs of God's church. On the positive side, God calls you into service, equips you with gifts, nudges you through his Holy Spirit, and may even push you into action.

Dr Hoefler loved to tell about watching a little boy helping his father rake leaves. The father had a wheelbarrow and would fill it with leaves and transport the leaves to the nearby fire. All the while the little boy would grab a handful of leaves, walk by his father, and deposit the leaves in the fire. The child was excited because he was helping his father. Perhaps you think it is a small deed but not so. I ask you a simple question. Will you dare to help your heavenly Father?

Day Twenty Five
Kingdom
Confidence

Reading: Matthew 13: 24-29

The fourth verse of Luther's famous hymn, A Mighty Fortress, states, "God's Word forever shall abide, no thanks to foes, who fear it; for God himself fights by our side with weapons of the Spirit. Were they to take our house, goods, honor, child, or spouse, though life be wrenched away, they cannot win the day. The Kingdom's ours forever."

Martin Luther wrote this hymn in the year 1529, although the date is uncertain. It is based on Psalm number 46. The hymn spread rapidly throughout Germany and it is reported that Luther sang it daily while in Coburg. There are over eighty translations in fifty three languages. The last line conveys Luther's steadfast belief in the power of God and also conveys in one line the basic meaning of the parable in Matthew 5; the Kingdom is ours forever!

The parable of the Wheat and the Tares is often unsettling for the simple reason that it appears to tell us to simply leave evil alone. I, and I know you too, find that troubling. Many of us want to take up our "weapons of the Spirit," as Luther calls them, and take on the evil in the world. And indeed there is a time and a place for combating the evils in the world. But Wait! Wait we are told when it comes to the weeds. What? You have to be kidding. Wait? That is what the parable tells us. It says that an enemy sowed weeds in the garden and the servants ask, "Then do you want us to go and gather them?" The surprising answer is No! The clear theme for us is this—the kingdom is ours forever. The wheat will ripen. The good guys will win. God will be victorious and of that we can be certain. That is what rings clear for God's people—the confidence of a certain harvest.

At funeral services Romans Chapter 8 is often read. It is a favorite of mine. Listen to Paul's confidence; "Romans 8:37-39 "No, in all these things we are more than conquerors through him who loved us. For I am convinced that neither death, nor life, nor angels, nor rulers, nor things present, nor things to come, nor powers, nor height, nor depth, nor anything else in all creation, will be able to separate us from the love of God in Christ Jesus our Lord."

Do you have weeds in your life? Are you troubled by persistent problems? Are you agonizing over a difficult decision? Some people rub their hands together in worry. You know the type, "Oh no, it just isn't going to work out." I will never be able to work at this new job. I do not know what to decide. How shall I start over with a friend I have offended? Isn't it human nature to imagine the worst case scenario possible? Isn't it human nature to live in fear, live in dread, and live in anxiety?

There are demons in the world and they assault us daily. The confidence of the Kingdom is also ours and it is this confidence that gets us through the day. It is Kingdom confidence that is ours in Jesus Christ. Make no mistake about it; it is not our confidence in our abilities, our reasoning, our great attitude or our positive thinking that keeps us on the right track. It is the confidence of Jesus Christ and His promise of the Kingdom. The wheat will be harvested. God will be victorious. Evil will be defeated—once and for all! Believe this, children of God—God will take care of you! Believe it!

Once upon a time there was an emperor riding through the countryside. He came upon a very elderly gentleman who was digging in the earth to plant trees. "Old Man" the emperor shouted, "Surely you do not expect to eat the fruit of the trees you are planting." "I have not given up that hope," the old man answered. "While I have my strength I will do my duty." "How old are you?" the emperor inquired. "I am 100 years old," the planter said. "God, who granted me longevity, may even allow me to eat of the fruit of these trees. But in any case when I plant trees I am merely imitating God's act of creation when he ordered that the earth bring forth fruit-bearing trees." "Promise me," the emperor said, "that if you are alive when these trees bear figs you will let me know."

Several years later when the trees produced fruit, the old man loaded a basket full of figs and made his way to the King's palace. When he arrived at the gate, he was initially refused admission, but due to his persistence and his old age, he was granted an audience with the king. "I am the old man you saw planting trees several years ago," he told the emperor. "I have brought a basket full of figs which I plucked from the trees you saw me planting." So pleased was the emperor with his gift that he accepted the fruit and ordered that the basket be filled with coins. Then he addressed the old man, "Go home good friend and continue to participate with the Almighty God in the act of creation."

When asked what he would do if he knew the world would end tomorrow, Luther replied, "Go and plant a tree!" This is Kingdom Confidence. The man in this story understands Kingdom Confidence. God will bring a harvest. Trust in God's power to bring about a harvest for you. So, why not plant wheat with the full expectation that God will give it growth.

Day Twenty Six
Two Face

Reading: Matthew 16: 13-23

Two Face! Can you imagine having a name like that? Tommy Lee Jones plays the character Two Face in the movie, Batman Forever. One side of his face looks normal and the other side is severely burned. Often, when we use the term, "Two Face," we refer to the behavior of an individual who exhibits two different personas. They present one face to this crowd and another face to that crowd. The individual has an opinion that is common to the people they are with and they might change that opinion another moment. Being "two-faced," as people say, means also breaking the commandment that says, "Thou shall not bear false witness against thy neighbor." To be two faced is to say one thing today and another the next day.

This is not a character trait that bodes well for life in the community of faith. And yet, look with me for a moment at someone who appears to be "two-faced." His name, you may know well. He is the disciple who said, "You are the Christ, the Son of the Living God." These words came out of the mouth of Peter, the disciple called the rock. Peter was the strong one. Peter was the leader of the early church and certainly some-one we admire.

Peter, the rock, however, was not immune to the cunning assaults of the devil. So do not think for a minute that you are immune from the sly tricks and maneuvers of the devil either. No more than five vers-es later Peter rebukes Jesus. Rebuke means to censure or admonish someone. In slang terms it might sound like, "shut up!" To rebuke someone is to be done only with great reserve. To rebuke another, according to the gospel of Luke, was only when someone had sinned and one rebukes them in a spirit of humility and to call them to repentance. Peter rebukes Jesus. One minute Peter confesses Jesus' Messiahship and the next he ex-presses great disapproval of Jesus' mission. Why would Peter do such a thing? Peter is the rock, but Peter is not the foundation.

Jesus explains his mission. It was to go to Jerusa-lem and suffer many things, be killed and on the third day be raised. Peter did not ask for clarification. Peter did not exercise active listening skills and say—Jesus could you say more about the being killed part—be-cause I do not understand. Rather, Peter takes Jesus aside and rebukes him. Two faced, that is what we call it and Peter fits the bill. Peter fails and fails miserably.

And guess who rebukes Peter—Jesus. Get behind me Satan! You are a hindrance to me; for you are not on the side of God, but of men. Jesus calls Peter—Sa-tan! Anyone who stands in the way of the mission of Jesus Christ is working with Satan.

The mission of Jesus is to suffer, die and be raised. The churches mission, and also your mission, to use the phrase from Mission Impossible, should you choose to accept it, is not much different. To be sure Jesus' death on the cross crossed out your sin once and for all and secured your eternal salvation. This is the good and gracious news of God. You too have a mission and it is clearly to be of one face.

The one face of the believer is to be the face of Christ. We are to look like compassion and forgiveness. We are to look like we are always and forever willing to lose our lives for the sake of others. Peter's problem was he wanted to put Peter's mission for Jesus in place of the real mission of Jesus. Peter forgot he was to be the rock and not the foundation. Peter wanted to put his wishes and his desires in place of the mission of Jesus.

Peter was to lose his face. He was to lose his mission in life for the sake of the mission of Christ. "For what will it profit a man, if he gains the whole world and forfeits his life?" We are to have the face of one willing to lose all for the sake of Christ. That is what we are called to do! Nothing less will do.

Many people wear crosses around their necks, some visibly and some hidden. A cross around your neck reminds you of whose you are and may be a gentle reminder against being "two-faced." But the call of God goes further than the call to hang a cross around our necks—in fact the call is to hang on a cross! Am I delusional? Did not Jesus hang on a cross so we would not have to?

Yes, Jesus did the work of salvation for us once and for all. But note what Paul says in Galatians 2:20, "I have been crucified with Christ; it is no longer I who live, but Christ who lives in me...." We are to have the face of Christ. We are to wear Christ's smile, Christ's love, and Christ's compassion. We are to subdue and spiritually crucify that which interferes with our full embrace of Jesus.

That is the challenge for you. At any moment we can succumb to the sly ways of the evil one. Peter confesses, "You are the Christ," and moments later rebukes Jesus. So, know that the devil lurks around looking for someone to devour, but stronger still is the power of Jesus. Get to know the mission of Jesus and understand your calling. Present through your face, the face of Christ!

Day Twenty Seven
Living in
Centralia

Reading: Luke 17: 11-19

The year was 1961 and the town was Centralia, Pennsylvania. I am told that some maps no longer show the town. A walk through this town today would reveal some homes, a Catholic Church, a few stores, and virtually no people. There are a few individuals still living there. Underneath this ghost like town is 24 million tons of Anthracite. The coal began burning underground in 1961 and is burning still today. Smoke seeps up from underneath and is seen all around. One gas station owner learned that 13 feet underneath his tanks the ground temperature was 1000 degrees Fahrenheit. The federal government tried all sorts of ways to extinguish the underground coal with no success. So in the year 1979 the Federal government used 42 million dollars to completely evacuate the town. There is a web site dedicated to the town reporting that a few people refused to leave.

Can you imagine with me for a moment what these people must feel like? Some had been on the land for generations and the land was literally burning before their eyes. The few people who remain must feel isolated and alone. They live in a ghost town.

Have you ever said to yourself, I want to get away to a deserted island, get away from it all? When the world closes in on you, responsibilities overwhelm, tasks seem too demanding, stress piles high; our first thought might be a nice secluded island. If you are a television viewer and you watch commercials you may have noticed that a major credit card company gave away an island. Do we, however, really want to be alone and secluded? Of course we do not.

You and I need to be among other people. We are created for companionship. That is why the scripture begins with a story of the relationship of two people. God said in Genesis 2:18, "It is not good that the man should be alone;" And so God created Eve. You and I were not meant to be alone. And yet, so many people feel disconnected.

Take a look at the story in this reading. The lepers lived in community with other lepers and yet they lived outside the camp. They were always on the periphery, always on the outside, and always away from normal interactions. They were disconnected from their families and disconnected from their faith.

Today, there are people living outside the camp, living in a symbolic Centralia. They are secluded, isolated, and yes, alone. They are disconnected. And they are sometimes us. There are times in our lives when we live in Centralia and feel disconnected. Divorce, death, transitions, and moving can elicit in us a feeling of being outside the camp.

The lepers, feeling a deep disconnection cry out from a distance, "Have mercy on us." That is our first cry when we feel alone and isolated, "Lord, have mercy on us." This is not so much a cry for help as it is also a cry for community. The lepers are saying, "Lord we are tired of being away from our families, tired of being outside the camp, and tired of being treated less than human." Because being human means living in the camp, being in community, being in partnership, being with the ones you love, and being with God's family.

If it wasn't enough that the lepers were disconnected; they were also disfigured. It is pretty common knowledge that the disease of leprosy left its victims with large sores that often distorted one's face and limbs. They were not only outside the camp where they felt isolated, but they looked different and as such were treated less than human. Jesus had mercy on them. He granted them healing and made them whole. They were restored as complete human beings. The leprosy was healed and there was no disfigurement and there was no more disconnection from their family and friends. This was a miracle.

All of us need such a miracle. We may not have a skin disease but we certainly have the sin disease. And this sin disease marks us not as a tattoo marks the body, but as a tainted mark on our souls. We are inwardly disfigured. We have guilt and shame, and are often haunted by the things we have done wrong. We live in the ghost town of sin. In spite of the fact that God made us for community; even though we want to be with others; although we long for a life soul mate; even when we yearn to be in the family of God we still experience broken relationships. It is as if we sometimes say, if only I lived on a deserted island. Truly it is hard to live in community.

But we were made for one another. God wants his people together. God wants to wrap his arms of mercy around you and include you and encourage you and make you whole. You do not need to serve on some church committee to belong. You belong. You are part of God's family and you are not alone because God is with you. He is with you through his word. He is with you when two or three gather in his name. He is with you through the sacrament of his body and blood. He is with you.

Ben Hur is a classic movie. In the closing scene in which Jesus hangs from the cross, rain falls down as it washes over the body of Jesus. The rain mingles with the blood of Jesus and flows into a leprosy camp. As it reaches the lepers, they are healed.

You and I are new people in Christ Jesus. Even with the scars of sin, even with the hurt of broken relationships, and even with the difficulty we often have in striving to live in community with others who are different from us, God brings people together. In fact, through the blood of Jesus Christ we are made whole and are made into the body of Christ. As a believer, you are a part of the body of Christ. You are the hands of Jesus. You are created to bring his healing to a fragmented world. You are called to be a part of a community of believers. Find a congregation, if you do not already belong to one, and live with and among God's people.

Day Twenty Eight
Touch a Tassel

Reading: Matthew 9

I wore a gold tassel on my graduation cap when I earned a Doctor of Ministry degree. Gold is used for doctoral degrees while black is the standard color for others. How many tassels have you noticed? Tassels are used in many places. For instance the Tboli women of the Philippines use tassels made of horsehair and beads to adorn a wedding hat. In Scandinavian myth, tassels made of acorns hang in windows to protect a house from thunder and lightning. In the 17th century, parts of the church used an Ecclesiastical hat from which tassels would hang. The Cardinal's hat was scarlet with 15 tassels on each side. Of all the uses and places of tassels there is also a biblical use.

Let's review the references in the Bible. Numbers 15:38, "Sew tassels onto the bottom edge of your clothes and tie a purple string to each tassel." Deuteronomy 22:12, "And when you make a coat, sew a tassel on each of the four corners." The gospel of Matthew makes a reference to tassels in Chapter 23:5, "Everything they do is just to show off in front of others.

They even make a big show of wearing Scripture verses on their foreheads and arms, and they wear big tassels for everyone to see."

Now that you have a background on tassels look once again at Matthew 9 verse 20. What does it say? Naturally, as with any text the translations differ, but the word used for the fringe of Jesus' cloak is the same word used for tassel. In fact the word fringe and tassel are interchangeable. What significance is there in this mere tassel? It shows that Jesus is wearing a cloak and the cloak has tassels as a reminder of the law. Jesus is a devout Jew who is following the custom of his people by wearing the proper garment.

This is where this story gets very interesting. The woman who has a flow of blood, thus she is unclean according to Leviticus Chapter 12, touches the fringe/tassel on Jesus' cloak. She touches only the tassels, the same tassels that remind us of the law. When Jesus turns to her he immediately says, "Take heart daughter, your faith has made you well." An unclean woman who is sick is made well by touching the hem or tassel of Jesus' garment.

Just as Jesus set the woman free from bondage to physical sickness, Jesus also sets us free from the bondage of spiritual sickness. Luther said that Jesus came to save and free us from the power of sin, death, and the power of the devil. Spiritual sickness is seen in the Pharisees. They turned religion into a show to pit one against another. They had tassels on their garment as the law required, but as Matthew writes in Chapter 23 they made their tassels long so as to draw attention to themselves.

The woman did not make a big show of touching the tassel. Rather, it was her hope that touching the tassel was enough to heal her. Contrast this with the Pharisee's religion of being showy. They displayed for all to see their big phylacteries and long tassels, as if to say, look at how holy I am. The Pharisees strict adherence to the law caused them to miss that the law was not a tool to build walls between people, pitting the "goodlies" against the sinners, but rather to teach all of us how to live together in community. The Pharisees used the law to set themselves up as better than others, whereas Jesus understood the law as a way to help us live our lives in community. That is why Jesus cites the citation from Hosea 6:6 and Micah 6:6-8 "I desire mercy, not sacrifice." Laws guide us in the best way to live together in community, but it is a law that must be administered with mercy.

The tassel was a symbol of that law, but it was not the tassel or the law that gave the woman healing. It was her faith in Jesus. Jesus gives healing to our bodies and to our souls. The law is merely a tassel when it comes to our relationship with God. We can know the law and know the Ten Commandments, but knowing Jesus and having a relationship with him is what transforms us. The law convicts us of sin and drives us to our knees seeking mercy. It is Jesus who grants us mercy. Jesus is the fulfillment of the law. Jesus gives us healing.

But once we are healed; once we have that strong relationship with God in Christ, we are not left alone. We are sent back to the law to see not only how we have fallen short, but once again to see the law as a way to live in the community of faith.

Now that you know all about tassels I suggest that every time you see one you remember the law God gave to his people. But I urge that you also remember the one who fulfills that law and grants healing to our bodies and our souls, Jesus the Messiah!

Day Twenty Nine
Can You Hear Me
Now?

Reading: Psalm 19

A poem by William Wordsworth depicts the beauty of creation and uses this line, "What wealth the show to me had brought." In the poem the inspiration of thousands of daffodils on the margin of a bay was deeply and emotionally moving. My childhood walks through my grandmother's flower garden often yielded as many as fifty different color variations of Daylilies. A walk outside on a bright sunny day will reveal to you a stunning patchwork of colors and natural beauty. All of it is the handiwork of God.

Most often we speak of seeing the creation of God. Interestingly enough, however, it is a different picture in Psalm 19. Reflect on these words, "The heavens are telling; the firmament proclaims; day to day pours forth speech; night to night declares knowledge; yet their voice goes out." What is striking about the language is that these are not word pictures, but rather an appeal to the sense of hearing. In other words, instead of looking at the creation and seeing the glory and the amazing handiwork of God, we are to listen to the creation. How does one hear creation?

Those of you who live outside the city and are surrounded by trees know what it means to enter in the city and hear anything but the creation. Listen and you will hear the hum of a motor, the buzz of a light, the boom of jets and planes flying overhead, and if you listen carefully, you will hear the noticeable low hum of an electric transformer. There is so much noise. No doubt the psalmist had no idea of such noisy interfering items.

And yet the psalmist invites us to listen. Listen and you will hear the heavens telling, the firmament proclaiming, the days speaking, the night declaring and the voice going out through all the earth. Perhaps we could simply suggest that the sound of a cricket, the call of a bird, the growl of a bear, the fluttering wings of a turkey, the sound of the wind in the trees, the babbling of a brook, and all other natural sounds are the result of the creation singing. The creation is God's choir. There are tenors, basses, sopranos, altos and who knows what else. And what is all the singing about? The earthly choir is praising God for his incredible glory and his immense creativity.

Now of course the psalmist says to us that there is no speech nor are there words; their voice is not heard; yet their voice goes out. The creation itself is not divine. There is no reference here to pantheism, no reference to nature religion. This is not about finding

God in nature, but rather that the creation is singing to us about the glory and wonder of God. Listen and hear.

But that is not all that speaks to us of God's great glory and wonder. The Law of the Lord also tells us of God's great glory. The psalmist uses six different words to describe the law of God. He writes that the law is perfect, sure, right, pure, true and righteous altogether. This is in stark contrast to the wisdom of man that is so often imperfect, unsure, sometimes wrong, always tainted by biases, sometimes deceptive and false and certainly not always righteous. In God's law we see the glory of God and the wonder of God. In fact there is so much wonder in this law and so much power that even the law has the power to do great things in our lives.

Note the words. The law revives our soul, makes wise the simple, rejoices our hearts, enlightens our eyes, is a greater prize than gold, and is sweeter than honey. The law of God sings as well and the notes bring joy to our lives. Like a good piece of music that soothes our souls so is the law of God. Listen to the law as it sings the praise of God.

Finally, the psalmist prays. He asks that God will clear him of faults, keep him from sins and protect him by not letting sins have dominion over him. The psalmist is praying that his words and his meditations will be acceptable. He prays that his words will be acceptable as an offering and acceptable as a means of praise. In other words the creation sings the praise of

God, the law sings the praise of God, and the psalmist prays that these words he has written will be his praise of God.

A popular commercial portrays a man walking in various places holding a mobile phone close to his ear. The man asks repeatedly a question that has burned itself into our consciousness. Do you know the commercial of which I speak? The question he asks is, "Can you hear me now?" I sometimes wonder if God might ask that question of us. With so much evidence that God is speaking to us how could anyone ask, can you hear God now?

Yes, the heavens are telling the glory of God. The law of God is perfect and in it we hear the key to life, wisdom, and joy. So listen carefully.

Day Thirty
Fishing Anyone

Reading: John 21: 1-19

It was a long time ago, but I remember it well. David promised me an adventure. He and I set out for Charleston S.C. early one morning. It would be my first experience in shrimping. We had trouble starting the boat motor, finally it started. We got about a half a mile into the marshes when the motor died. The adventure turned into a small nightmare, hot sun, smelly marsh, and only one oar! Like I said, some adventures one never forgets.

All of us enjoy a vacation. Vacations are like adventures because there is the thrill and excitement inherent in exploring, meeting new people, and seeing new places. I invite you on a remarkable adventure. This is an excursion that has been conducted for nearly two thousand years. It is the fishing adventure of a lifetime.

Jesus is the tour conductor. Jesus knows the best places and where the most fun will be and it all began on the side of a lake. A lake is a good place to start. Lakes have boating, fishing, sunbathing and the promise of great relaxation. This time the tour begins with some disgruntled men who had hoped to have a successful fishing expedition but instead they caught nothing.

If you have ever been on fishing trip and caught nothing you know the frustration. Take for instance the guy who goes fishing with a rod and a reel and one of those fake worms of any color. Compare with the guy who goes with a full tackle box with spoons, flies, worms, lures by the dozen and even something called fish bait spray. I have even seen the guys who have mapped out the lake and know all the right spots. Now, I ask you, who is going to catch the fish? The guy who is prepared is going to catch the fish. Me, well I am the one who drowns worms.

Who will teach us to fish? Jesus. Jesus gives us the tools. His tackle box is filled with lures by the dozen. The most important lure is love. Jesus attracts other "fish" (translation—people) by the power of his love. You have heard the old cliché you attract more bees with honey than vinegar! John's gospel states this theological principle in the twelfth Chapter verse 32. "And I, when I am lifted up from the earth, will draw all people to myself." Jesus' attraction is powerful enough to catch even the wisest and most evasive fish. It is Jesus power not mine, not yours, not some high powered evangelist that draws and attracts.

Jesus will teach us to fish. Jesus will teach us that luring with love is far more rewarding and productive. For years, the people of the church have used guilt to motivate and move people to action. This tool is of little use anymore. Besides, how can one look at the dying form of Jesus and see the love in his eyes and not be moved. The early church blossomed and grew in a hostile environment. Many people died because they dared to love Jesus. You are called to fish with love.

Maybe some of you are saying I do not want to fish. I do not enjoy it. But consider that this type of fishing, fishing for people is a real rewarding adventure. The reason people do not enjoy fishing is because they go at it halfway and halfheartedly. For many years when our family planned a trip we called AAA. We would get all the information necessary. We studied and planned what we were going to do. We built a reservoir of knowledge and anticipation. The same is true for our mission to fish. We need to learn, plan, and gather all the information we can and in so doing we will find it rewarding.

For instance, let's talk about the two components of fishing for people. First, there is catching. The fishermen thought they knew how. Jesus tells them to cast their nets on the right side of the boat and find fish. They follow Jesus' instructions and catch more fish than they can handle. If you want to be a successful fisherman then the first rule is to listen to Jesus. Jesus knows where the fish are. If you want to learn about tennis you would not call Michael Jordan. If you want to learn how to sing I don't think you would call Bob Dylan. When you want to learn how to fish and how to attract people to living an abundant, productive and wholesome life, then you learn from Jesus. You listen to Jesus.

Too many churches spin their wheels and accomplish little because they are fishing from the left side of the boat. Perhaps the church that is dying, long ago quit listening to Jesus. Maybe the traditions were more important than the word of the Lord. Maybe they forgot that it is the Lord's church and Jesus knows what will make the church thrive.

Some of you are going to be the catchers. You are the strong extroverts. Your job is to talk to people, listen to their needs and invite them to be in fellowship with other believers. We are not to go out and look for those most like us and then persuade them to come to church. The catcher's job is to look for people who are hurting, who are experiencing emptiness, and who are searching spiritually. The catcher's job is like that of Philip who said to Nathaniel "Come and See!" Most importantly, your reason for fishing comes from Jesus. What is the reason for going fishing anyway? It is fun and you love it. The same is true of fishing for people.

Jesus asks Peter three times, "Do you love me?" If the answer is yes, then the logical result is you will fish for others to introduce them to Jesus. You will become a catcher.

The second component is feeding. Jesus told Peter, Feed my sheep. Feeding is an important part of the adventure. You and I are privileged to feed the sheep. In other words, some of you may not be as good at catching, but you are real good at the feeding. To feed is to teach. To feed is to nurture. To feed is to care. To feed is to encourage. To feed is to listen. To feed is to love, love and love some more.

I remember my early days in ministry at Good Shepherd Lutheran Church in Swansea. It was a small congregation in a small town with an average attendance of about fifty people. What do you think happened when a visitor showed up? They were bombarded with love and warmly welcomed. Sometimes it scared people. But what they lacked in programs they more than made up for in feeding sheep.

Now, reflect for a moment. Are you best at catching or at feeding? Remember, Jesus stands ready to guide and direct you. This is a good time to assess your specific call. Will you catch or feed? This moment is a good one to make a concerted effort to fish. The fishing expedition with Jesus is a wonderful trip. Will you get on board?

Day Thirty One
A Band-aid Kind
of Love

Reading: John 15: 9-17

Ayoung man walked into a card shop. "I just want the right card for a special lady," he said. The clerk pointed to their best selling card. It said very simply, "To the only lady I have ever loved." "Terrific!" said the young man. "I'll take six of those!"

Too bad the idea of love has been so misused and misunderstood. Love is more than a card. Love is a commitment and a lifestyle. But more importantly, real love, true love is from God. In the reading for to-day, Jesus addresses the topic of love.

If you were asked to recite a passage of the Bible about love you might name the Great Commandment. "You shall love the Lord your God with all your heart, mind, strength and soul, and your neighbor as your-self." Or maybe you would call to mind the Golden Rule, "Do unto others as you would have them do unto you." (Luke 6:31) Few people, however, call to mind this text from John. Jesus tells his disciples, "This is my commandment that you love one another as I have loved you."

Truthfully, we know that love cannot be commanded. You cannot make someone love another person. That is why these words are so powerful. God's love comes first. We can love because God first loved us. This is not, however, a new idea or insight in scripture. The initiative of God is seen clearly in the Ten Commandments. Notice the words that come before the first commandment. Exodus 20: 2, "I am the LORD your God, who brought you out of the land of Egypt, out of the house of slavery." Prior to the commandments God stakes his claim on us and says, I am the Lord your God and this is what I have done for you; I brought you out of the land of Egypt.

In the New Testament Jesus tells us to, "love one another as he I have loved you." Jesus later demonstrates his love by accepting the fate of crucifixion. We remember the Golden rule, but not this passage because to love as Jesus loves is hard. This is love that lays down one's life. This is not an effortless love. This is not the kind of love that is sentimental and sweet. This is love that loves the loveless, cares for the uncaring, and turns the other cheek. This is hard love. But it is the only kind of love that lasts forever. The love of Jesus is love that has permanence and sticking power.

I remember a commercial about Band-aid brand bandages. The slogan was, "I am stuck on Band-aid because Band-aids stuck on me." One summer the youth at Lutheridge, a camp located in Arden, North Carolina, decided to turn that phrase into a Jesus jingle. It went something like this, "I am stuck on Jesus because Jesus is stuck on me." Maybe you think it is childish, but the simple truth is so profound. Jesus is stuck on you.

Jesus is stuck on you and he doesn't cover a sore here and one there. Jesus covers up our whole messy lives so that when God looks on us he sees only the beautiful righteousness and holiness of Jesus Christ. "No one has greater love than this, to lay down one's life for one's friends." Jesus laid down his life, once and for all, for all. The prophet Isaiah said it more beautifully than any other O.T. prophet. Isaiah 53:5, "But he was pierced for our transgressions, he was crushed for our iniquities; the punishment that brought us peace was upon him, and by his wounds we are healed."

Your life would be hopelessly lost and lonely without the powerful permanent love of Jesus Christ. It is only through the power of his love that we can truly love another.

A pastor reported about her nursing home visit with an elderly lady who had Alzheimer's disease. The family found those visits tough to endure. The daughter visited on this particular day with the pastor. Toward the end of the visit the daughter began singing Jesus loves me. The mother, though her memory was affected in many ways, sang along with the daughter with one exception. The refrain went like this, "Yes Jesus loves me, he always tells me so."

Jesus is telling you, "I love you." These are not empty words, but words filled with promise. Claim these words, believe these words, and live these words.

Day Thirty Two
Can You Believe It?

Reading: 2 Corinthians 4:1-6

Have you ever had one of those experiences where your only response is, "I cannot believe it." For instance an AAA truck driver told me about being called to assist a young lady who had locked her keys in a Jeep Wrangler. When he arrived he noticed that the Jeep had a soft top. A soft top Jeep has zip out windows. This particular Jeep had zip out windows in the driver's door and passenger's door. The AAA guy told me he could not believe it. The lady greeted him and said, "I have locked my keys in my Jeep." He unzipped the front window, unlocked the door, and secured the keys. Can you believe it?

Consider the story of Larry Walters. In July of 1982 Mr. Walters made a childhood dream come true. Known as Lawn chair Larry, Larry attached helium weather balloons to a regular lawn chair. Attached to his chair were drinks, snacks and a pellet gun to shoot the balloons and land his lawn chair aircraft. He expected to go about 50 to 100 feet in the air, but instead the balloons lifted him 16,000 feet into the air. He landed safely but was fined by the US Federal Aviation Administration. Can you believe it?

If you think those things are amazing and unbelievable consider this. We believe in a God who has no beginning and no end. God took a hand full of nothing, flung it across a vast openness and a whole world was born. God created the double helix of deoxyribonucleic acid, better known as DNA. Our greatest minds do not fully understand the intricate and amazing rungs of the DNA ladder. God created a universe that is millions upon millions of miles across. God created everything and continues to create. God created you and me. Can you believe this? Do you believe this?

God visited earth in the fullness of his Son Jesus Christ. Anthony Flew, a philosopher, said that if there were a religion that he could believe in, Christianity has it all. But like Flew and so many others, Jesus, is often the stumbling block.

It is difficult, if not impossible to believe, that Christ Jesus is the likeness of God. It is difficult, if not impossible to believe, as Paul writes to the Colossians that in Christ the fullness of deity was pleased to dwell. Can you believe this? Do you believe this?

The truth is I cannot believe it, nor can you believe it, on your own. But we believe it because our eyes were opened. The veil was lifted from your eyes, because you cannot lift the veil on your own. You and I cannot believe that an all knowing, all present, and all powerful God would visit earth. It is hard to believe

God loves you and me fully and completely. But believe it I do, because God lifted the veil and activated my faith. In the same way, God activates faith for all persons through faith and through hearing the word in preaching and through baptism.

One of my parishioners used to say, "It is impossible for me to believe that there is a God, let alone believe that he became a human being." But, he believed it. Why? He believed because God activates faith. Lutherans adamantly and repeatedly defend Luther's explanation to the third article of the Creed. Luther wrote, "I cannot by my own reason or strength believe in Jesus Christ my Lord or come to him; but the Holy Spirit has called me by the Gospel, enlightened me with his gifts, sanctified and kept me in the true faith."

The Holy Spirit wants to lift the veil from our eyes and help us see. The Holy Spirit wants to usher us into a new realm of seeing, a new way of believing, and a fresh way of living. Faith makes a difference in our lives. Can you believe it? Do you believe it?

We want to believe fully and completely. But you and I also know that our days are often filled with doubt and struggle. We know that it is not easy to live the good news of Jesus Christ. We know it is not easy to follow Jesus. It is not easy to believe and trust in Jesus. It is not easy to yield our wills, our minds and our whole selves to the rule of Jesus Christ. You and I know the "gods of this world" want to blind us to the truth. We know the gods of greed, the gods of lust, the gods of envy, the gods of jealousy, the gods of narcissism and all the other gods can and will distract us from Christ, destroy our love of Christ and demolish our faith in Christ. But we also know, we also believe, we also trust that these worldly gods, these worldly ways that blind us to truth have no power over us. Can you believe this?

Our power to believe, our strength for daily living and believing comes from God. "I believe that I cannot by my own reason or strength believe in Jesus Christ my Lord." I can believe these words. These are comforting words. These words mean that you do not have to muster up more faith to please God. You do not have to climb the rungs of some mythical ladder of faith so as to get closer to God. You do not have to earn your way to God's heart of love. You do not have to exhibit super faith. You cannot lift the veil from your eyes to see, really see God at work in your life. But God can lift the veil.

I walked all morning along the Appalachian Trail and was looking forward to the afternoon stop at Clingman's Dome. Clingman's Dome is a 6,700 foot mountain. On top is a man made concrete ramp. I arrived at the dome eager to see the breathtaking view. Climbing to the top we were surrounded by fog and could see nothing. I sat there for what seemed like forever and then there was a break in the clouds. I could see. It was breathtaking. Some people say you can see seven states from this place. For a person of faith, it was not a view of states, but a panorama of God's majesty.

God can help you see in a new way. The faith we need to see is the faith God gives. God gives us new eyes of faith. God gives you strength for daily living. God opens your eyes to see the presence of the Messiah, Jesus, in your life. Paul writes, "For it is the God who said, "Let light shine out of darkness," who has shone in our hearts to give the light of the knowledge of the glory of God in the face of Christ." This means that you can believe in Jesus. You can believe in Jesus' power in your life. You can believe tomorrow will be exciting and filled with promise because the light of Christ is shining in your life. Can you believe this? Will you believe this?

Day Thirty Three
Where Demons Dwell

Reading: Luke 4:1-11

John Ylvisaker captured the hearts of many when he wrote the song, "Borning Cry." This beautiful hymn says that God is present at our birth, present as we age, present at our baptism, and even present when we wander off where demons dwell.

Have you ever wandered off where demons dwell? It is the place where your inward gut tells you that this is a place you should not be. It is a place of lies. It is a place of gossip. It is a place of manipulation and deceit. It is the soft voice that tempts a teenager or adult to enjoy an illegal drug, for there is no real harm in it and you will not hurt anyone. It is a place of evil. These places, however, are easy to find. It is even easier to dismiss that there is any real evil.

Our contemporary scientific minds downplay the concept of demons. We think of them as mythic creatures holding pitchforks with horns atop their heads. But demons are real forces that destroy people and their lives.

Demons have a prominent role in the New Testament as adversaries of Jesus and as agents of the master Demon, Satan himself. There are accounts in the New Testament in which Jesus casts out demons. Take for instance Mark 1:23, "Just then a man in their synagogue who was possessed by an evil spirit cried out..." Or for instance verse 32, "That evening after sunset the people brought to Jesus all the sick and the demon possessed."

My son Mark and I attended the movie Gran Torino, which, if you can withstand the onslaught of horrific vulgar Language, has powerful biblical imagery. The movie portrays gang violence. As he and I discussed the evil of violent gangs, I reflected once again on the reality of unbridled evil in the world, the kind of evil that places no value on human life. Need we recount the scenes from Auschwitz where at least 960,000 Jews, 75,000 Poles, and some 19,000 Gypsies were killed? A vivid and moving account is depicted in the classic book by Eli Wiesel—Night.

The point is clear; evil is loose in our world. But for us the real evil seems so far away as perhaps to be unreal. But evil is pervasive and shows up in unexpected places at every opportunity. Immediately after Jesus' baptism, the Spirit sends him out into the desert for forty days to be tempted by Satan. The temptation ends with these lines, "the devil left him (Jesus) until an opportune time."

Jesus is baptized, not because he was sinful, nor because he needed to repent, but to conquer the power of evil once and for all. The scripture says that the baptism of Jesus is "to fulfill all righteousness." To fulfill is to complete and all righteousness is the will of God. This means that Jesus is baptized to complete the intention of God. And God's intention is to seal each of us in baptism with a protective cover, a permanent presence of the Holy Spirit to guard us.

God cannot guard you against the onslaught of temptation and the soft voices that lure you away from truth, but God can protect you from being totally consumed and destroyed by evil. God does this through baptism and by connecting you to Jesus Christ. Jesus stood toe to toe with the fullness of evil for forty days.

An illustration will help. Think of a bookend as an appropriate image for baptism. Bookends are those physical props that are positioned at both ends of a rack of books. Bookends hold the books upright. Our lives are bookended by Jesus. The churches season of Epiphany season illustrates this concept of being positioned between two bookends.

God says after the baptism. "You are my son, the beloved; with you I am well pleased." God announces for all to hear that Jesus is the son of God. Jesus is loved by God. God is pleased with Jesus.

At the end of the Epiphany season is Transfiguration Sunday. On that Sunday of the appointed reading is, "This is my Son, whom I love, listen to him." Note the similarities. "You are my son, the beloved;

with you I am well pleased." "This is my son, whom I love, listen to him."

In other words, at the highpoints in the earthly life of Jesus, his baptism and his transfiguration, the voice of God shatters the quiet and says, "You are my son and I love you...." These points in the life of Jesus serve as bookends to his life.

Your life is marked at the beginning and the end by Jesus. Jesus is the bookends of your life. Jesus helps to hold our lives upright. When you took your first breath—the Lord Christ was present. When you were baptized—the Lord Christ was present. As you grow older—the Lord Christ is present. When you wander off where demons dwell, the Lord Christ is present. Jesus is the bookends of our lives. We are on earth to write a story with our lives.

I invite you to reflect on the power of Jesus in your life and then to write a story of love and of positive values. Live knowing that the power of God's spirit dwells in you and with you in every place you go.

Day Thirty Four
A Parking Place
Jesus

Reading: Matthew 16:13-28

Have you ever told God what you wanted or what you needed? Sure you have, if you have ever prayed before it is highly probable that you asked God for something. Ponder for a minute what it might mean if we decided to tell God how to do something. The conversation might go something like this, "Dear God, I realize you have a lot to do and are watching over a lot of people, but I need you to help me every day as I go to work to find the best possible parking place. That way I can save a little more time and of course, spend more time in prayer!"

I am certain you can spot all the flaws in this logic. To suggest God is interested in me, or anyone else for that matter, finding the best possible parking space, is silly. Joseph Sittler in his classic book, Gravity and Grace, tells the story of a parishioner who asked God for a parking place and God did not answer her prayer. She told Dr. Sittler about her misfortune and

God's lack of an answer and Sittler told her that the first family, Mary and Joseph, did not get a parking place either, but spent the night in a stable.[14]

How daring it is for anyone to tell God what to do or to presume to know better what God should do. This is the case with the apostle Peter. Jesus spells it out. He tells his disciples that "he must go to Jerusalem and undergo great suffering at the hands of the elders and the chief priests and scribes, and be killed, and on the third day be raised."

Now I must admit that had I been present to hear these words, I, like all the others would have been shocked. Peter, bold one that he is, is the first to speak, "God forbid it, Lord! This must never happen to you." This is the same guy, Peter who six verses before says, "You are the Christ, the son of the Living God." Imagine that. Peter confesses that Jesus is the Messiah, the one the prophets foretold, the son of the living God, and then six verses later tells God's only Son "no."

No, I forbid it Lord you will not suffer. You will not be killed. You will not be raised? Would he dare to change the plan or will of God? Would you? When have you wanted to change God's plans? What exactly are God's plans? While part of God's plan is for us to have abundant life, this does not always mean that we get everything we want. It does not mean that everything will go our way either.

Consider one popular televangelist whose private jet and lakeside mansion as well as a host of other interests gives his extended family much wealth. Or another popular preacher who said, "I think God wants us to be prosperous." Or another who said, "I believe God wants to give us nice things." Michael Gerson writing in the Washington Post and reflecting on the "Gospel of Wealth" wrote, "Whatever ethical problems such leaders may or may not have, they face a large theological challenge. A religious system that promises happiness and "nice things" is difficult to reconcile with the faith whose founder had "no place to lay his head," urged his followers not to store up "treasures on earth," and called on them to deny themselves and take up a cross of suffering.... And in this odd faith where the poor in spirit are blessed, the highest ideal is suffering for others—though most of us do precious little of it. This model of spiritual leadership has nothing to do with conventional measures of success and influence."[15]

It is God's plan for us to love him and to demonstrate that love in service and love for other people. We follow God's plan by doing our jobs to the best of our ability. We follow God's plan by serving God's church. We follow God's plan by being hospitable to all people. We follow God's plan by looking to the needs of others.

At the 100th anniversary of the arrival of missionaries in Zaire, Christians gathered to celebrate from that part of Zaire once called the Belgian Congo. The festivities lasted all day with music, preaching, food and conversations. Many reminisced about the early days and praised God for the progress of the gospel and the church.

Near the end of the long program, a very old man stood to give a speech. He said that he soon would die and that he needed to tell something that no one else knew. If he didn't tell, his secret would go with him to his grave. He explained that when the first white missionaries came, his people didn't know whether to believe their message or not. So they devised a plan to slowly and secretly poison the missionaries and watch them die. One by one, children and adults became ill, died and were buried. It was when his people saw how these missionaries died that they decided to believe their message.[16]

It was the way they died that taught others how to live! Take up your cross and follow Jesus wherever he may lead you.

Day Thirty Five
Only a Baby?

Reading: John 1: 1-14

Sarx! Dr. Hoefler said this word with a fierceness that was unmatched. Sarx is the Greek word for flesh. The Word became flesh. This word was Jesus. Jesus became flesh. Think of the meaning of that simple little verse. God became a human being. The infinite creator God chose to clothe himself with flesh.

A minister's association celebrated Christmas with a breakfast meeting at a local restaurant. The group shared what the incarnation, the idea of God becoming flesh in Jesus, meant. Each minister shared meaningful insights and comments. Some offered sermon possibilities. It was, however, a woman in the group who pointed out the frailty of a little baby in a manger. Someone, she said, had to change his diapers, someone had to feed the baby Jesus, and someone had to hold him, swaddle him, and protect him.

Why would God dare to let us, his fallen creatures, people who brought about the banishment from the Garden of Eden, a humanity that became so wicked that God sent a flood to destroy the earth, hold him, and diaper him? God did this, in a word, to be vulnerable. Vulnerable according to Webster' dictionary means, "Capable of being physically wounded."

This is a baby who in the words of the famous hymn Silent Night is a "holy infant so tender and mild." The baby Jesus is tender and mild, vulnerable. He is capable of feeling pain, capable of smashing his finger with a hammer, and capable of crying. This Jesus, vulnerable baby, is our God.

My parents love to tell this story on me. It was Christmas and I was one of the three wise men. At the appointed time in the pageant, I and two other boys walked down the aisle and placed our gifts near the manger. My parents tell me, however, that my curiosity overcame me. Caught up in the moment, I leaned over and stretched out as far as I could to see what was in the manger. Apparently, I was a bit disappointed when I reached inside to discover nothing more than a hard plastic baby doll.

Are we disappointed at what we find in the manger? This is Jesus who is a mere baby, tender and mild. Most often we stress the divinity of Jesus. We talk of his power, his miracles, and his resurrection from death, but what about his humanity, what about his frailty? What does it mean to us that our God became like one of us?

When we meet and experience Jesus Christ, fully human and fully divine, we are never the same again. The Christ child came to bring peace and joy. Those who truly look at the baby Jesus can never really hold a grudge and can never really whine and complain about the hardships of life. God in flesh means God is in the midst of us. God in flesh means that the sweet little baby suffered an excruciating death. Jesus felt the pain. Jesus felt the nails. Jesus felt the abandonment of God. He was deserted, forgotten, emptied, and powerless. Jesus the sweet baby was the crucified child of God.

What does it mean that Jesus is human? It means God is in the midst of our hurts and pains working constantly to make all things new. Jesus is the sweet little baby. He is the baby who brings peace and good will to you. Will you dare to trust him?

Day Thirty Six
A Devilish
Holiday?

Reading: Ephesians 6:10-18

Let us pretend this morning for a moment that one of you decided to go for a stroll along the beach. It is a warm day and the sun is shining brightly. You walk out on to the beach for a stroll. The date is June 6th. As you walk along you see and hear the sounds of war. And before you know it you are in the midst of one of the most discussed battles of all history. You are on the beach outside Normandy, France.

While it may seem a stretch to some, there is a battle being waged every day. The battle is not fought with weapons of war—tanks, guns, and grenades, but with the slick and sinister temptations of evil. Evil is real. Evil is powerful and evil is present at every turn; perhaps even more so for the Christian. And like our pretend stroller on the beach of Normandy, many Christians go about their day in a nonchalant way as if there is no war.

And yet we are so often naïve. We want to believe and trust that all is good and all is right with the world when under our noses lurks the very things which would devour us.

Luther wrote, "The devil takes no holiday; he never rests. If beaten, he rises again. If he cannot enter in front, he steals in at the rear. If he cannot enter in the rear, he breaks through the roof or enters by tunneling under the threshold. He labors until he is in. He uses great cunning and many a plan. When one miscarries, he has another at hand and continues his attempts until he wins."[17]

Are you afraid? You should be. This is no post-enlightenment mythology. It is no laughing matter, but very real. I often think that one of the reasons I hold to faith in a living and loving God is because of the very real presence of evil.

Paul argues in Ephesians 6:12, "For our struggle is not against flesh and blood, but against the rulers, against the authorities, against the powers of this dark world and against the spiritual forces of evil in the heavenly realms." Paul recognized and named evil. Evil assaults the truth. Evil assaults righteousness by holding up to you all your sins and driving you to a place of despair. Evil distorts the gospel and turns it into a feel good salve that does not demand repentance. Evil tells us that faith is merely wishful thinking. Evil tells us that the Word of God has no real relevance for today and is just one book among many. Evil tells us that our prayers do not matter. Evil assaults constantly and as Luther wrote, "continues his attempts until he wins."

For you see you will fail. You will succumb to the inner voices that tell you to ignore the needs of your neighbor or look the other way when injustices prevail. All too often we nonchalantly laugh at evil as if it is not real or it does not affect us. We fall to the pride that says, in the words of a pop psychology—I'm Ok and you're Ok. We are not Ok. We are sinners and we are in the hands of a cunning and diabolical force. Call it the devil. Call it evil, but do not treat it lightly or you will find yourself in darkness before you know it.

Nathaniel Hawthorne describes the journey of Goodman Brown and his step by step walk into a place of evil. Hawthorne writes, "With this excellent resolve for the future, Goodman Brown felt himself justified in making more haste on his present evil purpose. He had taken a dreary road, darkened by all the gloomiest trees of the forest, which barely stood aside to let the narrow path creep through, and closed immediately behind. It was all as lonely as could be; and there is this peculiarity in such a solitude, that the traveler knows not who may be concealed by the innumerable trunks and the thick boughs over head; so that with lonely footsteps he may be passing through an unseen multitude."[18]

The journey to evil begins with but one step and it often seems so alluring. But Paul writes, "Be strong in the Lord and in his mighty power." (Ephesians 6:10) Andy Bolton is a physical strong man who held the world record in the raw dead lift having lifted 1003 pounds. Have you ever wondered about the training these men and women must do? Failure to train for a dead lift will cause a literal crushing effect on the spinal discs. But these men and women train with every ounce of their being.

   Why is it any different for you and me? It is not. God asks that we put on God's armor. God's armor will make us strong, but we cannot set it aside for one moment. We live in it at all times. God's armor will never fail you. Christ is with you every moment of every day. Put on the full armor of God and feel the protection.

Day Thirty Seven
Time to Come Home?

Reading: Luke 15:11-32

What exactly is it like to be an older sibling? Are you the eldest in your family? The first born boy or girl has a unique role in the family. First born children blaze the trail and either make it hard or easy for the siblings that follow.

Suppose you are the first born son and you work in the family business. You work alongside your father laboring long hours to make the business thrive. And the business does thrive. But your younger brother will have none of it. He decides to find himself, as we are so often prone to say—whatever that means. So, while you labor away, younger brother pleads with his father to allow him to have his inheritance now.

Now we know that your father is a generous man so he gives his consent and writes the check. This is a small family business so Dad writes a check by mortgaging his home—again. The younger son is given 250,000 dollars, his share of the family business.

After a trip to Hawaii, a cruise to the Mediterranean, a shopping expedition to the Mall of America, the purchase of a new 6000 square foot home Ocean front home at North Myrtle beach, giving money to all his friends and family who want to help him with his "Extra" money, and, of course, a new Maserati Gran Turismo with all the options and a price tag of only 135,000—(what a deal), the younger son discovers, much to his surprise, that he has no money left.

He does not even have enough cash to buy a Big Mac Extra Value Meal—super sized! The young squanderer realizes that the bills will come due and he is broke. Now what will he do? In desperation he goes back home and expects to get what he deserves, a job raking manure out of the horse barn! Instead his Father runs out to greet him and throws a large party. His father spends money like a mad man and welcomes the younger son, your brother, back into the fold. And, in essence, forgives your brother all of the debt. Your younger wasteful brother gets full rights to all the family, to all the family love and, of course, back into the family business.

And so you, the older brother, the one who blazed a trail of efficiency, strong work ethic, and wholesome living, see this taking place. How do you feel? Do you think such thoughts as—what is fair is fair and this is not fair? Do you ponder how this will affect the business and the cash flow? Do you entertain a small tinge of jealousy, anger or frustration? Do you question your father's kindness, compassion, and forgiving attitude?

This is no new story, but a story that plays out nearly every day. The prodigal son is greeted by his loving Father, but there is always an older sibling. The older sibling is the one who is always there and always productive and faithful. How would you feel? Is it fair for this amount of debt to be forgiven? Is it fair to the other who is left behind and given his life to being dutiful while the younger son lives foolishly? Should he not get his just reward?

We often act like older siblings. Many of us have been followers of Jesus for decades. We tend the field of faith while others wander around searching for answers and seeking purpose. We give to the church while others casually toss a dollar in the plate at Easter or Christmas. We do our duty, fulfill our commitments and work diligently in the field of faith. And when one wanders in from the streets of squandering, what do we do but begin to judge.

And while we are being so dutiful, what does our Father do? All the while our heavenly Father waits patiently and lovingly for one of His profligate children to return.

And when one straggler returns, our Heavenly Father does not dole out judgment or send them to the barn to rake manure, but welcomes them with arms of mercy. Who is this waiting Father who would do such a thing? After all, do we not expect some consequences, some punishment to be exacted to pay for this reckless younger brother? Who is this God that would behave in what seems to the older brother such a careless way?

This is your God. This is the God who recklessly gave up his only son on the cross. This is the waiting Father who patiently watched as Roman soldiers pounded nails in his son's hands and feet, pierced his side with a spear, planted a crown of thorns into his scalp, and humiliated him until he drew his last breath.

Oh yes, make no mistake, there are consequences to our immoral behavior and our shameless ways. The punishment the younger brother deserved and that we deserve was put on Jesus. This is your God—Jesus—who hangs from a cross demonstrating that no matter how far you wander, how recklessly you live, how foolishly you spend your life in endless pursuits, God waits with open arms and an open heart.

Yes, it is true; the punishment you and I deserve for our recklessness, Jesus took upon himself. God wants us in the field of faith working for his kingdom. Your Holy, Heavenly Father is waiting for you.

Day Thirty Eight
A Maze of
Mirrors

Reading: John 10:1-10

Remember the house of mirrors? You could see them at fairs and carnivals. The mirrors provided confusion and deception making it difficult to find your way. Yes, the maze of mirrors was merely one way to have fun at the fair, but it is this event which provides a metaphor for life. Life is a maze of mirrors.

We bounce into the world as babies without a choice of when we will be born or where. While I did not choose to be born in the state of South Carolina and the country the United States with all of its opportunities; that is the way life began for me. What about you?

Once we enter the world an abundance of choices are presented to us. Multiple paths are before us. A multitude of doors appear in our future. Many distractions exist to detour our efforts. Where will we go and what path will we choose? It is easy to become confused. It is deceptively simple to walk the wrong path.

Sometimes we hear a voice calling. We listen but do not recognize the voice. The sound may be pleasant, soothing and inviting, but we sense something is wrong. Many voices call to us when we wander through the maze of life. Nearly everyone is trying to sell you happiness, wholeness, health and fulfillment. They cry out to be heard. Read this book and you will find meaning and purpose. Follow this regimen and you will lose weight and find happiness. Spend a week in Vegas and you may come home rich. Listen and you will hear many sounds. Look and you will see many mirrors deceiving you.

We are not called as Christians to hear all the voices, but to listen and hear only one voice, the voice of God. We are not called as Christians to follow many paths, but one path, the path of faith. How will we find our way through the maze of mirrors? Jesus. Jesus opens doors. Jesus is the door. Jesus gives life, abundant life, and full joy for living day to day. Though the reflections we see deceive us and while we may get lost from time to time, Jesus never leaves us. He lays down his life for us. He provides a clear direction. His voice is always recognizable. We find our way to life, abundant life, through Jesus.

He is not merely a model of morality. He is not simply a terrific teacher. He is not one path among many. Jesus is Messiah. Jesus is God. Jesus is the one and only son of God who died and then rose from death.

His way is the way to find what life is really all about. But some came before him and many have come after him who ultimately, whether overtly or not, seek to kill and destroy. The message of the Messiah is twisted by some, distorted by others, and even maligned by many. But the message of Jesus to give us a better life stands the test of time. In many ways the fundamental message of Jesus shows up in fiction literature, though not always so obvious.

The books we read illustrate our hunger for new life, new adventures and our search for meaning. The all time best-selling book series is the work of J.K. Rowling—Harry Potter. Four hundred million copies of her works have sold. These novels display choices and the raging battle between good and evil. There are subtleties in her work that depict meaning and fulfillment in life. Another best seller—The Lion, The Witch and the Wardrobe is a fantasy fiction that clearly portrays the message of the Messiah.

These two works of literature plus so many others illustrate that we hunger for meaning, adventure, fulfillment and abundant life. All of which come to fruition in the Messiah. We want to have a life filled with adventure, filled with fun, filled with meaning and hope. And even though we live in a maze of mirrors where it is easy to get lost, the Messiah will make himself clear to you.

While life will always be filled with many choices and many voices beckoning you to come here or there, the church exists to bring one clear choice and one clear voice, the Messiah, Jesus Christ. You hear his voice in the gathering of God's people in worship. You are given his body and blood in bread and wine to fill you and nourish you. Jesus came to give you abundant life. Jesus is abundant life. His path, his voice, and his teachings are truly the one way to find your way.

Day Thirty Nine
Playing With
Pennies

Reading: John 10:28

Do you remember a special game you played as a child? What are some of those games? Think for a moment about them and the joy you had in playing. There was one I recall from my high school days called the pennies game. It works like this. One individual holds a hand full of pennies while another places their hand over the pennies. Then, the fun begins. The object of the game is to snatch the pennies out of the hand below before it closes. If you are able to snatch a few pennies you are a winner.

Allow me to paint for you a picture of life as the pennies game. What are the treasures you hold in your hand? What are the pennies? Make a list. Our gifts are life, faith, eternal life in Christ, and if the list continues it should include all of our treasured relationships. Note too that the gifts can include tangible things that we own, but I would suggest that those gifts are not nearly as important as our relationship with Jesus our Messiah and our relationships with one another.

So here we are, you and I, holding in our hands the gifts from God. People of faith are supposed to look at those gifts, cherish those gifts, and give thanks for those gifts. It is true, however, that we often take these "pennies" for granted. Instead of seeing them for the treasures that they are, we treat them as mere pennies and maybe even act as though they are not that important.

Suppose you woke up one morning and slapped your hands together and said loudly, "Good Morning Lord." What would your spouse think? Perhaps more often your morning shout is, "Good Lord it's morning."

We can easily slip into turning each day into another blah day instead of seeing our treasures. Why do we do that? Perhaps it is because the world and our sinful self, that old Adam nature that haunts and harasses us all, steals our joy and snatches from us an attitude of thankfulness and appreciation. So we hold these treasures, but not tightly enough so that our appreciation of what God has given and continues to give is taken from us.

The world is a place where someone is always looking to snatch your joy and valued treasures. Maybe not intentionally, but that is the way it is. In the church we call it sin. Sin is looking out for number one. Sin is coveting your neighbor's stuff. Sin wants what someone else has and it is forgetting to cherish what God has given you. And instead of an attitude of gratitude we develop an attitude of snatching. We forget to give thanks for what we have and begin to look in the hands of others and want what they have. Naturally, none of us have ever done that! Surely, you have never coveted your neighbor's car or house or job or other belongings? Yes, we all have. What if you decided to cherish your gifts from God? What most important gift do you have? Is it your relationship with Jesus Christ? Is he your salvation, your most important cherished treasure?

What if you could know with certainty that no one could ever take from you your most valued treasure? Would that not be comforting? Jesus uses the word snatch. He says, "My sheep hear my voice, and I know them, and they follow me; and I give them eternal life (our greatest shiny penny), and they shall never perish, and no one, shall snatch them out of my hand."

Do you see? Nothing can take you from the hand of God. Nothing can pry you from the Good Shepherd—Jesus Christ. Nothing can snatch you from the loving and caring embrace of the heavenly Father. God holds you tightly. Jesus is your Good Shepherd and he protects you from the wolves that would steal your joy and strip away your gifts. Jesus the Good Shepherd protects you. Breathe a sigh of relief. Think of what that means. You belong to Jesus. You are his sheep and he holds you tightly in his embrace.

While on a guided tour of the Holy Land the passengers on the bus had been told time and time again that the shepherd never drove the sheep like cattle, but always walked in front, leading them. As the bus

168 REV. TONY A. METZE

came around a curve they looked out the window and saw a herd of sheep being driven by a man. The tour guide was clearly flustered and stopped the bus. He went over and had an extended conversation with the man driving the sheep. He returned to the bus with a triumph smile on his face as he announced to the tourists, "He's not the shepherd. He's the butcher!"

Jesus, the Good Shepherd wants to lead you. Will you trust him? Will you rest secure in his protective arms of mercy knowing that nothing can snatch you from his grip of grace?

Day Forty
To See Jesus More
Clearly

Reading: John 14:1-14

Have you ever faced a difficult and challenging situation and someone offered you unsolicited advice? Say for instance you are facing an uncertain future, whether it is job prospects, economic uncertainty, or an illness and someone offers these words, "You need to be strong." Now while those words may be offered with compassion and concern and while those words may even seem encouraging, how do they make you feel and do they truly help? "You need to be strong." This sounds good and has the potential to help, but it falls short.

Why do these words fall short? They offer only one part of the solution. Compare the aforementioned advice to this one, "Let not your hearts be troubled." Is there any difference? No, at least when taken alone. These words, however, do not stop there. The entire phrase is, "Let not your hearts be troubled, believe in

God, believe also in me" These are not mere words; they are God's Words. In other words when we are facing challenges in our lives we hear God say to us, that no matter what the challenge, God will be with us and promises us a better day in eternity. God promises us a place. There are many mansions in God's eternal home.

But there is more for us. God's promise does not mean we have to wait for strength, wait for encouragement, or wait for eternity. The presence of Christ is with us now. The holy and powerful presence of Jesus, who is the way, the truth and the life is here to guide us and comfort us when the challenges seem overwhelming. The trouble begins, however, because of doubt and disbelief. We may say we believe, but we practice doubt.

There is a story of a congregation in a farm community that held a prayer service for rain in the middle of a drought. There was not a cloud in the sky the morning of the prayer service. But one parishioner came with an umbrella. When asked why, his simple reply was clear, "Are we not praying for rain?"

Do you believe in God and believe that Jesus is the way, the truth and the life? Do you believe that he is with you, but do you practice your belief? Do you carry an umbrella when you pray for rain?

The dialog between Philip and Jesus sounds like many of our conversations in prayer. Ever had one like it? It might go something like this, "God, are you listening? And if you are, why are you allowing these pretty harsh troubles in my life? I thought you were

strong. I thought you were the Creator. I thought...."
You can fill in the blank as I know all of us have had
these prayerful conversations.

Philip asks to see the Father as if that will make
everything better, but gets this response from Jesus,
"Don't you believe me Phillip look at the works themselves." Jesus invites Phillip to open his eyes to see Jesus clearly. Get to know Jesus, really know Jesus and
then practice belief in Jesus.

This is not easy. We cannot merely mouth any
words and throw up some short prayer expecting God
to do a powerful work in our lives without some strong
passion and desire on our part. We need a deep longing
for God.

As a youth I sang the song entitled, Day by Day.
There were three requests; to see thee more clearly,
love thee more dearly, and follow thee more nearly.
This sums it up very well. If all who profess belief in Jesus sought to see, love and follow him, most churches
could quit doing half of what they now do and take up
more meaningful Kingdom work. The church, however, often finds other things to distract it from its primary and main mission.

Today it seems that much of Christianity is ob-
sessed with a lot of things. Somewhere in the mix we
have lost something. Dr. Yeago in his comments on
the blog, Lutherans Persisting, said it like this, "We
lack energy. Despite the best of intentions, our message is often pretty thin—too often alternating between a small gospel of therapeutic comfort and a soft
legalism of vaguely-imagined service. Jesus figures in

our speech too often as either the consoler who makes us feel better about life's stresses and hardships or the example we ought to be following as we too go out and redeem the world."[19]

As one parishioner often said to me, "we got to keep the main thing the main thing." We hear a lot about social justice and the work of doing advocacy for the hungry, all of which has its place. But it is not the main thing. Much of Christianity worries about every special interest group and their feelings and less about the redemptive life changing power of Jesus. This causes me to ponder if we really believe that Jesus is the way, the truth and the life.

While I understand the challenges of living in a pluralistic society and the need for Christians to be hospitable and kind and to engage in interfaith dialog, this does not mean, however, Christians should promote a bumper sticker theology that suggests we coexist and go along to get along. To do so is to deny the radical nature of the gospel which calls us to share the message of Jesus. To make disciples is to help people see Jesus clearly; to see that Jesus is the Messiah and the Son of the one and only Living God. Either Jesus is the way for all people or he is simply another god and that is god with a little "g."

To see Jesus is to see his works and to see his works is to do his works. Jesus said it plainly, "Very truly I tell you, whoever believes in me will do the works I have been doing, and they will do even greater things than these. And I will do whatever you ask in my name." (John 14:12-14)

Is this not practicing faith? Doing greater works? Is this not something more than paying lip service to the Lord who loves us? Ask Jesus to give you strength and then practice your daily life as if Jesus heard you. I invite you to cultivate a longing for God. Generate the deep desire for a relationship that is more than a mere passing fad, but a deep and abiding love for Jesus. Live in faith, dispel all doubt and carry an umbrella when you pray for rain, and of premier importance love Jesus. Is that not what you really want?

A Concluding Thought—What If Christ Was Raised?

It was a wedding reception and I was conversing with a few folks. A gentleman approached me to share his spiritual journey. He spoke about his new purpose in life with Christ, his new found joy and his hope for a brighter future. I asked him, "Have you ever thought how profound it is that as Christians we believe that Jesus Christ died and then three days later really and truly rose from the grave?" He stammered for a moment, gave me a very puzzled look and then proceeded on about his life and his hopes. I did not mean to derail this man or cause him angst; I merely wanted him to think beyond himself and his life. While I fully believe that Jesus came to give us abundant life, what if we focused a greater majority of our energy on pondering the profundity of resurrection? What does it mean that a man died and then rose from death in a glorified body that walks through walls and eats fish by the seaside? Do we engage in Docetism and think that he really did not die, but faked death? Do we secretly think that those disciples were really hallucinating or at best spiritually seeing Jesus, whatever that means?

As a result of an overemphasis on the historical—critical method of biblical study, an all out theological assault through such scholars as Rudolf Bultmann has sought to downplay and demythologize Jesus' bodily resurrection. N. T. Wright in his voluminous work, "The Resurrection of the Son of God," provides the most thorough orthodox treatment of resurrection in which he underscores the empty tomb and the appearances of Jesus as the only plausible explanation for what happened. I find it noteworthy that the world's most well known atheist, Antony Flew has changed his mind to Theism. In his book, "There is A God," he includes an appendix written by none other than N.T. Wright about, what would you guess, the resurrection of Jesus Christ.

If Christ was not raised, then we might as well close all of our churches and spend our money on more fruitful pursuits. As the Apostle Paul said, "If only for this life we have hope in Christ, we are of all people most to be pitied." (1 Corinthians 15: 19) But if Christ was raised from the dead, then all of history is changed forever. It might be entirely possible that American Christianity with its "therapeutic moralistic deism,"[20] has accepted a Bultmann theology. We are using Jesus for our pursuit of pleasure or profit because deep down we doubt the reality of the resurrection. But what if we believed it fully and completely? Would it not change our church programs and our style of sharing the good news of Jesus?

At one of my most recent Easter Sunday morning worship at St. Paul's Lutheran Church, I made a very concerted effort to pound like a nail the idea of resurrection. During the entire order of worship and many times in the sermon I said, "Christ is risen!" I coached the congregation to say, "He is risen indeed, Alleluia!" We said it so many times a few broke into joyous laughter. But is that not what resurrection is, a laugh at death and a smirk on our faces at the devil? For if we truly believe that Jesus conquered death through his resurrection, and then as our meager faith clings to him, we too have the glorious promise of life in eternity. How and why I cannot answer, but I suspect that since God made our DNA in the first place, he can rewire it so that there is no more pain, no more disease, and no more death. God can tweak our DNA to paradise perfection.

What if we decided to believe with full passion the power of the resurrection of Jesus Christ? Debunk all mythological approaches and accept several simple premises. First, Jesus died a real death. Second, Jesus rose from death in a body that walked through walls, but also ate fish. Third, Jesus appeared in bodily form to many people, people like you and me. Will you believe this? Will you allow this powerful news to take root in your life and shape you in new ways? Will you realize with your will, intellect and emotion that the

Holy Spirit can grant you this faith? Believe it and live it. The forty days are over, but the journey merely begins.

Endnotes

1   You can access his remarks at www.sclutheran.
     org or at www.lutheranspersisting.wordpress.
     com

2   Michael Horton, Christless Christianity, Grand
     Rapids: Baker, 2008, p.68

3   Horton, p. 70

4   Olie Hallesby, Why I Am A Christian, Minne-
     apolis: Augsburg, 1930, p. 133

5   Richard Niebuhr, The Kingdom of God in
     America, New York: Harper and Row, 1959, p.
     193

6   Hallesby, p. 54

7   Dr. Seuss movie, The Grinch Who Stole Christ-
     mas

8   Henri Nouwen, Reaching Out, New York: Dou-
     bleday, 1975, p. 46

9   Odyssey, John Sculley, page 90

10   Ronald Browncigg, Who's Who in The Bible,
     Volume 2, New York: Bonanza Books, 1971, p.
     141

11   David Buttrick, Preaching on the Resurrection,
     Religion in Life—Autumn 1976, Volume 45, No 3
     p.281

12   Catch 22, 450

13   David Buttrick, 281

14   Joseph Sittler, Gravity and Grace, Minneapolis: Augsburg, 1986, p.40

15   Michael Gerson, Washington Post, August 6, 2008, A:17

16   Leith Anderson, Winning the Values War, Minneapolis: Bethany House, 1995, p.198

17   What Luther Says, Concordia Publishing House

18   X. J. Kennedy and Dana Gioia, Literature, Pearson- Longman, 10th Edition, Young Goodman Brown, 549

19   Dr. David Yeago, Lutherans Persisting, www.lutheranspersisting.wordpress.com, accessed 29 May 2011

20   This is a phrase coined by Michael Horton in Christless Christianity